Computers and Information Processing for Business

Computers and Information Processing for Business

Microsoft Office 2019 and Python

Dr. Sergio S. Ribeiro

BEP

BUSINESS EXPERT PRESS

Leader in applied, concise business books

Computers and Information Processing for Business: Microsoft Office 2019 and Python

First published in 2020 by
Business Expert Press, LLC
222 East 46th Street, New York, NY 10017
www.businessexpertpress.com

ISBN-13: 978-1-95253-860-5 (paperback)
ISBN-13: 978-1-63742-328-8 (hardcover)
ISBN-13: 978-1-95253-861-2 (e-book)

Business Expert Press Information Systems Collection

Collection ISSN: 2156-6577 (print)
Collection ISSN: 2156-6593 (electronic)

First edition: 2020

10 9 8 7 6 5 4 3 2 1

This book is dedicated to my wife and daughter.

Abstract

This book is an introduction to computers covering relevant topics that include: computers and society, the Internet, social media, Microsoft Office 2019, and high-level programming. The main goals are to help students to define computers and information processing and describe the main concepts related to hardware, software, and their use. Also, it aims to prepare students to identify how the Internet has changed people's lives and develops critical thinking about the role of computers in society, recognize the impact of technology in the personal and professional base, to mention a few. Emphasis is placed on developing skills in Word processing, spreadsheets, presentations, and programming algorithms.

Keywords

Computers; computers and society; hardware; software; Internet; e-mail; Microsoft Office; Word; Excel; PowerPoint; Python; programing language; problem-solving; digital firm; business; business process; business routines; business skill; business career

Contents

Prepublication Reviews

"There are many books that could be used to teach an introduction to computers and electronics. Having spent almost three decades as a leader in business, I am refreshed that someone finally realized the need to teach introductory programming as part of that curriculum. With the growing prevalence of AI and Machine Learning applications in business, it is more important than ever that graduates into business environments be prepared to understand and perform the skills traditionally associated with programming. These skills are critical for all sorts of problem-solving and are widely missed by current introductory computer courses." —**Don Poort, CPA, Assistant Professor of Business Administration, Briercrest College & Seminary, Canada**

"It's a great book that describes the computer basics in a very easy and interesting way to the reader. It starts from the very basic concept of computer evolution and goes on to describe the very latest Cloud technology. The book accomplishes to provide basic insights into some key computer fundamentals like Networking, Operating Systems as well as Programming languages. I liked the fact that it includes hands-on projects as examples to the readers— all in all, a great book that can benefit a range of audiences from students to professionals." —**Vishal Arora, MCA, Sr. Technical Account Manager, Microsoft, Canada**

"Dr. Ribeiro provides a basic but powerful description of computers, social media, the Internet, Microsoft Office 2019 and high-level programming. The different interface of the digital firm, IT infrastructure, network and application are clearly elaborated and summarized in key points that help readers obtain a better insight on the information system's impacts on businesses. The step-by-step guidance is written in a friendly, welcoming manner that makes this book easy to follow, especially readers who are from a non-IT background." —**Alex Cheing, PhD, Assistant Professor of Business Administration, Briercrest College & Seminary, Canada**

"*This book is helpful for anyone who wants to learn how computers work, and processing the information, connecting different experiences and practical examples. The friendly and smooth approach offers a strategic content view with highlights on the contextualized connections and examples, an easy way to keep students and readers focused and interested. The structure adopted is learning easier, growing complexity as moving forward, clarifying the subjects step by step and converging, in all chapters, into the Review Questions, a suitable learning method. Professors and Students with interest in how Computers process the information, discussing relevant and current thematics such as the Digital Firm or Cloud computing, will find useful answers in this very well structured textbook.*"— **Alex Rosenbrok Teixeira, PhD, Department of Indigenous Science, First Nations University of Canada**

"*As an entrepreneur, I know very well how important is an excellent base in computer skills for business. In this book, Dr. Ribeiro covers the essential topics to give this base. To be honest, this book goes beyond when introducing the readers to the Python programming language. It is easy to follow, and has lots of practical examples. Indeed, it is an excellent book for anyone who wants to know how computers work in a business context. This book proves Dr. Ribeiro's experience and commitment to education and teaching.*"
—Fabio Maleta, Entrepreneur, Fix Coffee, Canada

Foreword

Students, in this rapidly changing technological world of too much information, need experts who can serve as steady guides to lead them through this technological revolution.

In one of my first meetings at Chapters with Sergio Ribeiro, I thought we would have a short meeting to discuss his essential philosophy of business practice. Instead, we had an in-depth conversation, nearly two hours long, about history, philosophy, culture, and books. It was apparent to me that Sergio was one of those *steady guides*. While schooled in business and technology, his deep interest surrounded the way in which technology, computers, and artificial intelligence were tools—tools that need thoughtful and careful use by those who wield them. Sergio's reflections about life and work derive from a concern for the world, and not just the latest trend or best practice in business. He is a devout family man with a sincere faith. His principles and teaching come from deep reflections that are heartfelt and tested in his own life and mind.

Sergio has one foot firmly planted in the technological world, with his other foot entrenched in business operations, research, and strategic thinking. With his international experience, being raised in Brazil, he has a perspective that sees past the malaise of North American materialist culture. He believes that computers and technology should ultimately serve the needs of people, communities, and cultures.

This past year, I was in a reading group with a number of faculty members, exploring the philosophy and practice of impactful teaching. Very consistently, Sergio's comments to the group would be focused on his reflections about the needs of students and the ways in which ideas and concepts need to be shaped for student learning. As a teacher, he strives to be student-focused with generosity, but not lightness. Rather, with clarity as his strategy, he strives for depth and excellence in his students.

Sergio has written this textbook as a clear and precise guide for students. It is not overburdened with technical language, jargon, or dense explanations. The material is student-centered, with concise descriptions for the novice. Nonetheless, this book will teach the essential and vital skills necessary for our technical workplaces. This book is not intended for the computer scientist, but the business student who needs the right collection of technical skills and knowledge to be successful in the business realm. The material has been shaped and selected with this goal. One of the distinctiveness of this textbook is the final section that teaches the basics of computer programming using Python—a very suitable platform.

While the world of computer technology is vast and growing, this textbook is crafted with the eyes of business operations and outcomes. I commend this book to students who need these crucial skills for the demands of our highly technical business world.

Don Taylor, DTh
Provost and Dean of the College
Briercrest College and Seminary

Acknowledgments

Every good gift and every perfect gift is from above, coming down from the Father of lights with whom there is no variation or shadow due to change

—James 1:17

CHAPTER 1

Let's Get Started

Learning Objectives
- Discuss computers and society today
- Reflect on the presence and impact of technology in our lives
- Understand the importance of learning about computer

What is your computer make and model? How do you use it? How many things do you do using your computer? How many hours do you spend on your computer every day? Are you happy with your computer, or do you think that it is time to get another one?

According to Webster, a computer is a programmable usually electronic device that can store, retrieve, and process data (Merriam-Webster.com Dictionary 2020).

My first contact with a computer was some years ago, and I was around ten years old at that time. I remember to be amazed by that machine. "That's so cool!" I said. "How does it work?" I asked. That time a computer used to be a little different than it uses to be today (Figure 1.1).

Figure 1.1 TK 85 personal computer from Microdigital

Source: Microdigital

I know the computer in Figure 1.1 looks like more a keyboard than a computer. However, believe or not, it was a little PC (Personal Computer) in the 80s. This PC was a clone of the English Sinclair ZX Spectrum, and its integrated motherboard had a Z80 processor, 16k of RAM, no hard disk, used a B&W TV as a monitor, a cassette recorder as a data storage unit, and an external power font. No Internet, Wi-Fi, Bluetooth, touch-screen, or any other modern technology default in most computers today. But, I remember having a lot of fun coding games in the BASIC programming language.

Quite different, my first daughter's computer was an Android tablet 7-inch, touch-screen, Wi-Fi, 1GB RAM, USB ports, camera, and audio.

If you ask your parents or grandparents their first computer, probably will be surprised by the technology of that time. In the old years, we used to have less technology around us.

Nowadays, computers are everywhere! There are computers in TVs, phones, coffee-machines, wash-machines, door-bells, elevators, fire-alarms, lamps, watches, cars, and so on. Yes, they are everywhere, easing our lives (See Tech Article: The Smart Home and Our Connected Life).

Eventually, we could just ignore the presence of computers around us because they became so prevalent. However, the purpose of this book is to discuss the importance of computers for the personal and business base.

Tech Article: The Smart Home and Our Connected Life

Figure 1.2 Our connected life

Source: NewsUSA

(NewsUSA)—Almost everything today is digitally connected … whether at home or on the go. Connected technology saves you time with everything from smart phones to smart homes!

Tech Lifestyle Expert Carley Knobloch has partnered with KillerApps.com and four brands for a look at some great smart tech for 2019 that will help simplify your life.

First up … a laptop is a must! Made for today's mobile multi-taskers, the thin and light Yoga C630 combines the power and productivity of a Windows 10 laptop with the always-on, always-connected mobility of a smartphone thanks to integrated 4G LTE and Wi-Fi support. Powered by Qualcomm's Snapdragon 850 Mobile Compute Platform, the Yoga C630 gets up to 22 hours of local video playback and features a natural pen-on-paper experience on its vibrant 13.3-inch FHD IPS touchscreen display with optional Lenovo Pen and Windows Ink.

Next, to stay connected at home, Orbi Voice is a smart speaker integrated with Amazon voice assistant, Alexa and uses the Qualcomm Wifi Mesh platform to create expansive whole home Wi-Fi coverage (up to 4500 square feet) to create an entire ecosystem of mesh Wi-Fi products. It also features premium audio technology, creating incredible room-filling sound from the audio experts at Harman Kardon.

Alexa makes it easy to play music from the most popular streaming services, control other IoT devices, check traffic, weather, and so much more—without needing a separate device. It's truly an innovative leap, and the start of a trend expected to accelerate in the 5G era.

Smart products can also help keep families safe. Fire is getting faster, but you can get ahead by installing Kidde Wire-Free Interconnect Smoke Alarms in your home. Kidde's new interconnect alarm solution offers exceptional safety benefits without the hassle of hardwiring or a Wi-Fi connection. The interconnect technology helps alert you to a fire no matter where you are in your home. When one alarm senses a hazard, all interconnected alarms sound throughout the home. The alarm also comes with a sealed 10-year battery, which you don't have to worry about changing alarms batteries. Simply replace the entire alarm after 10 years.

Home security solutions are getting smarter and more convenient too. Schlage Encode is the newest connected device to enhance the brand's portfolio of innovative smart locks. The deadbolt is easy to install, with a quick connection to in-home WiFi, making it even more convenient for homeowners to have secure, remote access control. The built-in Wi-Fi technology eliminates the need for an additional hub and allows users to set-up and manage the lock via the Schlage Home or Key by Amazon apps. This means users can lock and unlock their deadbolt, monitor the lock's status, and send virtual keys to trusted friends and family, all from the convenience of their smartphone. Homeowners can create up to 100 unique guest access codes for temporary, recurring or permanent access. This information, along with the lock's activity, can be tracked and monitored within the app, giving homeowners greater peace of mind. Through the Schlage Home app, users can also pair their deadbolt with Google Assistant and Amazon Alexa. When managing the lock via the Key app, users can enjoy compatibility with other platforms such as Amazon Cloud Cam, Ring video doorbell and cameras, and Alexa.

For more information, visit KillerApps.com.

Because computers are becoming more powerful, smaller, and affordable each year, more and more companies can invest in more technology. Computers play an essential role in business today, helping organizations to be more efficient and competitive. Investing in technology, companies can do more with less.

However, being the technology more and more present in the workplace, companies need professionals well qualified. Those professionals need more skills related to computers to manage and operate business functions efficiently throughout modern technology. Therefore, to succeed in a professional career today needs much more than being just a computer user. What you need to do is fundamentally understand how to use computers as a professional tool.

Understanding and getting a comprehension of computers as a professional tool is the purpose of this book. This book will help you to go through the fascinating study of computers. Learning about computers is awesome!

In the next chapters, you will see and understand how computers are made of, the concept of hardware and software, networking, the importance of the Internet today and its issues. Also, you will learn how to use the Microsoft Office for most of business daily routines, solving problems with a programming language, and much more.

If you get this book for your college class, your professor will define in the syllabus the order of chapters to be studied. However, if you would like to study in advance or if you got this book to learn by yourself, you do not have to consider the chapters in sequence. It is a technical book, not a novel or fiction book. So, you can go forward and back studying first those chapters that you interest more.

Take time to reflect, write down your notes, do the exercises, and assignments. Ask your professor every time you doubt about some specific point.

Summary

- Computer as an electronic device has been used for people from different generations
- Computers are present everywhere and have been employed for various purposes like study, work, and entertainment, to mention a few
- Because computers are primarily used for companies to improve business, it is crucial to develop computer skills for professional career success

Review Questions

1. List the computers you have in your house
2. Do you think computers are essential for people today? Why?
3. Why is it important to learn about computers?
4. Does being a computer user is enough for a professional position in a company?

Case Study: The Importance of Computers and Technology for Society

It does not matter what industry we are discussing. Technology is typically the backbone of all trades. It has become the thing that society needs because it is the way that information is stored. You can see below some aspects where computers have impacted our lives.

- *Shopping*—Consumers shopping at stores see how technology plays a part in their check out process. Others that are shopping online are also familiar with the way that a computer allows them to buy things without leaving their homes. This aspect has made technological innovation significant.
- *Innovation*—People are very dependent on the concept of technology that moves the world forward. They are excited about changes that society can embrace to communicate, work, and entertain.

- *Workforce*—The workforce is much more efficient with computer-based applications that are used to simplify a lot of processes that would be very time-consuming for humans. People are also able to telecommute and connect to video conferencing regardless of where they live. This possibility makes it much easier for workers to get jobs that can be done from home.
- *Entertainment*—Another thing that society depends on is the available entertainment. It is undoubtedly easier to stream music and movies with all the high-tech gadgets and smart devices that exist.
- *Health care*—It is even easier to treat patients in hospitals when information about their medical history can be accessed instantly. The advances in the tech world have made this possible. There are a lot of machines that can diagnose issues related to patients suffering. The health care world is better, and health information systems are the reason for this.
- *Data*—Available data allow all of these different concepts to work in a much more effective way. Information can be stored and retrieved from the cloud instantly from anywhere.

Case Questions:

1. List more areas where computers have been changing our lives and explain how?
2. List the pros and cons of being so dependable on computers?
3. Why do you think we are so dependable on computers?

CHAPTER 2

The Digital Firm: Computers and Information Processing

Learning Objectives
- Learn the importance of computers for the firm
- Describe computers
- Explain how a computer works
- Describe the evolution of computers
- Discuss the role of computers in the firm
- List the various types of computers devices used in business

In the previous chapter, we discussed the importance of computers nowadays and how they have eased our daily life. One main goal of any organization is to be able to "do more with less." It is the principle of efficiency, and computers have an essential role in allowing companies to simplify or reduce processing and get more results.

If we look at any company today, the attempt to find any daily routine that can be executed without the use of a computer is a tough task (Figure 2.1). Almost everything played every day for any organization will include some use of computers. If some process still exists executed without the use of a computer, probably someone is trying to find a way to automate that process.

Figure 2.1 *Computers are commonplace in today's business routines*

Source: Pexels

It is not new for us how vast is the employment of computers in almost every daily routine in organizations. However, someone could ask: How our lives became so influenced and dependable on computers? To answer this question it is necessary to understand at least the computer history, its evolution, how it is made of, and how it works.

Describe Computers

In Chapter 1, we already learned a computer is a programmable electronic device. It means a computer is an electronic machine able to receive instruction regarding how to work or what to do. The concept of a computer is pretty simple, based on the systems theory. It is a theory used to explain how groups of objects work together to produce some results. A system can be represented by the input-process-output (IPO) model (Figure 2.2).

A computer is a system that receives information from the input, processes that information, and returns the output as a result. The IPO is a simple way to represent a computer through a model. However, the *information processing cycle* (IPC) is a complete form to describe a computer system.

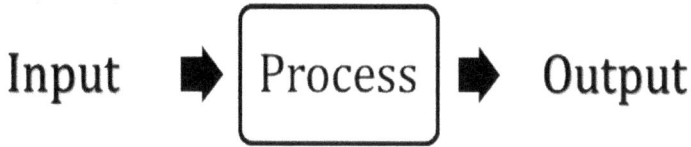

Input ➡ Process ➡ Output

Figure 2.2 System

Explain How a Computer Works

The IPC model can be used to describe how computers work once the model is based on four steps that are *input, processing, storage,* and *output.* As an electronic device, a computer is a machine that converts data into information. Data is a widespread collection of facts and figures that are generated all the time. When you contextualize your facts and figures, you have information. So, information is data processed, calculated, classified, and organized.

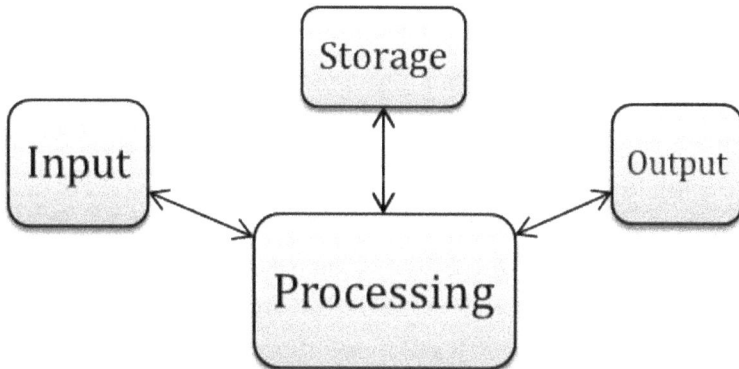

Figure 2.3 IPC model

As demonstrated in Figure 2.3, in the IPC model, each step can be described as:

1. **Input:** In this initial step, raw data is entered into the computer.
2. **Processing:** The input data is processed, calculated, classified, manipulated, or organized.

3. **Output:** The information resulted from the processing step is returned to you (to the computer user). Usually, the information is presented on a screen, printed in a paper, or in any other way.
4. **Store:** This information is then saved as a digital file format for later use.

When you go to a grocery store to shop for some products, eventually, the price of a specific item could not be clear. Maybe because the label on the shelve is not clear, the label was missed, or the product was moved to another place. In this case, you can get this item and go to a near scanner and scan the bar code to get more information about this product. In this example, the bar code is data that you can input into the scanner. The scanner device will process the input data and access a stored database to find more information about the product. Once the item was found, the information will be printed into a screen.

Facts and figures for us could be numbers, letters, symbols, or any other character. There are many languages around the world with a different writing system. The English language is based on the alphabet writing system that uses symbols to represent all sorts of individual sounds. However, other languages like Korean, Japanese, Arabic, or Hebrew have their language based on different writing systems. What about computers: which language do they speak? Is there a specific writing system used by computers?

Computers are electronic devices, and they speak electrical pulse. Basically, the computer writing system is based on two symbols that are *on* and *off*. Therefore, *on* or *off* is a computer data and for simplification, we can refer to them as *0* or *1*. It is called *bit* the smallest unit of storage. At this point, we can say that computer language is based on a *binary system*.

How could we use the binary system to store our type of data? Alphabet system is composed of many symbols, and 0 or 1 could represent only two symbols from the alphabet. For example, 0 could represent the letter *C* and 1 the letter *T*. However, if you want to store the word CAT using this system, you cannot. The system is limited to only two possible representations, not three. What about expanding the system using two bits to represent a letter? In this case, we could have something as demonstrated in Table 2.1:

Table 2.1 Binary code for two digits (bits)

00	C
01	T
10	I
11	A

In this case, the word CAT could be represented by the binary sequence 00 11 01, and we could store the word TIC as 01 10 00. Can you imagine how many symbols from our alphabetical system we could represent using a binary combination of 8 bits? It is how computers store information today. Each symbol, from any language around the world, is represented by 8 bits, also called *byte*. So a byte is a unit of information storage. How many bytes do you need to store a letter, picture, sound, or movie? Instead of talking only in bytes, we can use the units listed in Table 2.2:

Table 2.2 Binary code for two digits (bits)

Unit	Abbreviation	Definition
Kilobyte	KB	1024 bytes
Megabyte	MB	1,024 KB or 1,048,576 bytes
Gigabyte	GB	1,024 MB or 1,073,741,824 bytes
Terabyte	TB	1,024 GB or $1,024^4$ bytes
Petabyte	PB	1,024 TB or $1,024^5$ bytes
Exabyte	EB	1,024 PB or or $1,024^6$ bytes
Zettabyte	ZB	1,024 EB or $1,024^7$ bytes

By using the current computer binary system to represent data, it is possible to store trillions of bytes. You can use the ASCII table to find the equivalent binary code for a character.

Based on the ASCII table, the word CAT is stored in the computer as 01000011 01000001 01010100. This sequence of bits and bytes is how the computer says CAT.

Do you know how to write HELLO in binary code?

0	0011 0000	O	0100 1111	m	0110 1101
1	0011 0001	P	0101 0000	n	0110 1110
2	0011 0010	Q	0101 0001	o	0110 1111
3	0011 0011	R	0101 0010	p	0111 0000
4	0011 0100	S	0101 0011	q	0111 0001
5	0011 0101	T	0101 0100	r	0111 0010
6	0011 0110	U	0101 0101	s	0111 0011
7	0011 0111	V	0101 0110	t	0111 0100
8	0011 1000	W	0101 0111	u	0111 0101
9	0011 1001	X	0101 1000	v	0111 0110
A	0100 0001	Y	0101 1001	w	0111 0111
B	0100 0010	z	0101 1010	x	0111 1000
C	0100 0011	a	0110 0001	y	0111 1001
D	0100 0100	b	0110 0010	z	0111 1010
E	0100 0101	c	0110 0011	.	0010 1110
F	0100 0110	d	0110 0100	,	0010 0111
G	0100 0111	e	0110 0101	:	0011 1010
H	0100 1000	f	0110 0110	;	0011 1011
I	0100 1001	g	0110 0111	?	0011 1111
J	0100 1010	h	0110 1000	!	0010 0001
K	0100 1011	I	0110 1001	'	0010 1100
L	0100 1100	j	0110 1010	"	0010 0010
M	0100 1101	k	0110 1011	(	0010 1000
N	0100 1110	l	0110 1100	)	0010 1001
				space	0010 0000

Figure 2.4 ASCII table

The word HELLO converted into binary code is 01001000 01000101 01001100 01001100 01001111.

We do not have to convert words into binary code to work with computers. It is not a kind of skill usually required to apply for a business position in a company today. However, it is interesting to understand those units like bytes, KB, MB, GB, and so on. The reason is that computer storage and processing capacity is measured with those units. Updating computers in general means replace equipment with another one, and it is done based on storage capacity and processing power measured in bytes.

Describe the Evolution of Computers

The computer was born by 1880 in the USA to solve a severe number-crunching crisis. At that time, with the growing population, it took more than seven years to have the Census results tabulated. The government found a way to solve this problem by using punch-card based computers developed by Charles W. Seaton (Zimmermann 2017). However, in 1837 the first mechanical-general purpose computer proposed by the English mathematician Charles Babbage was described (Figure 2.5). Some authors consider Seaton's device, the first computer, and rather others believe that Babbage's machine was the first one.

Figure 2.5 Analytical engine of Charles Babbage

Source: U.S. Army Photo

In computer history evolution, there are lots of milestones based on each advance and disruptive new technology. Some notable events to be mentioned are the introduction of ENIAC the first multiuse computer

(1946); the invention of the transistor (1947); integrated circuit (1958); the mouse ("bug") developed by Douglas Engelbart (1968); microprocessor Intel 4004 (1971); first personal computer Altair 8800 (1974); Microsoft (1975); Apple II (1977); IBM-PC (1981); 3D printer (1983); Macintosh (1984); CD-Rom (1985); World Wide Web (1990); iPod (2001); and iPhone (2007) to mention a few. However, another way to see the computer evolution is to break down its development in terms of computer generations (Figure 2.6).

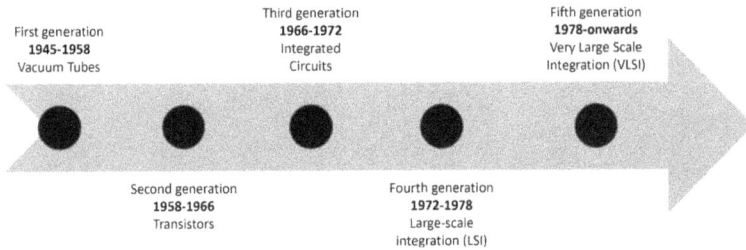

Figure 2.6 Computer generations timeline

The most important lesson we can learn from computing development is that it has been growing day by day. This evolution is to such an extent that it is almost impossible to mention all the advances we have achieved in recent years. Computers are getting smaller and less expensive every day. The perspective to the near future is the possibility to build robots that may have the capacity to understand and learn like humans.

Discuss the Role of Computers in the Firm

Working in a company today, you have to handle a variety of computer systems. Because technology systems are changing so fast, you have to know how to keep your computer system updated. Can you imagine how a firm could operate today without computers?

Modern technology helps the firm to be more efficient. Also, it is an essential tool for assisting managers in administrating better business processes. A company, to be competitive in the business market today, needs to be well equipped with the proper technology. Years ago, acquiring computer systems was expensive, and only big corporations were able to do that.

Information technology is continuously evolving, however, decreasing the price and increasing performance. Moore's Law explains this phenomenon. This Law states that we can expect double the speed and capability of our computers every two years, and pay the same amount of money for them. Also, because of the advent of the Internet, companies today can be global, expanding their business.

According to Webster, *ubiquitous* means existing or being everywhere at the same time. Also, *ubiquitous* comes to us from the noun ubiquity, meaning presence everywhere or in many places simultaneously (Merriam-Webster.com Dictionary 2020).

Today thanks to modern technology, products and services are available within easy reach of our hands. A smartphone is as little as our hand but is so powerful. This small computer allows us to do almost everything, everywhere, and at any time. Therefore, it is ubiquitous.

List the Various Types of Computers Devices Used in Business

You can find several different computer systems in a company. Usually, companies integrate those computers into a corporate network. There are different uses for those devices like editing documents, data storage, printing, file sharing, and so on. An employee in the sales department can use a desktop computer to access orders and check stock availability or even client credit. A manager going to a meeting at the supplier headquarter can use a mobile device to check the sales report. Computer systems allow employees to get access to the information from inside or outside the company network.

A personal computer (PC) is a small multipurpose computer with a microprocessor designed for use by one person at a time. Examples of PCs are desktops, laptops, smartphones, and tablets.

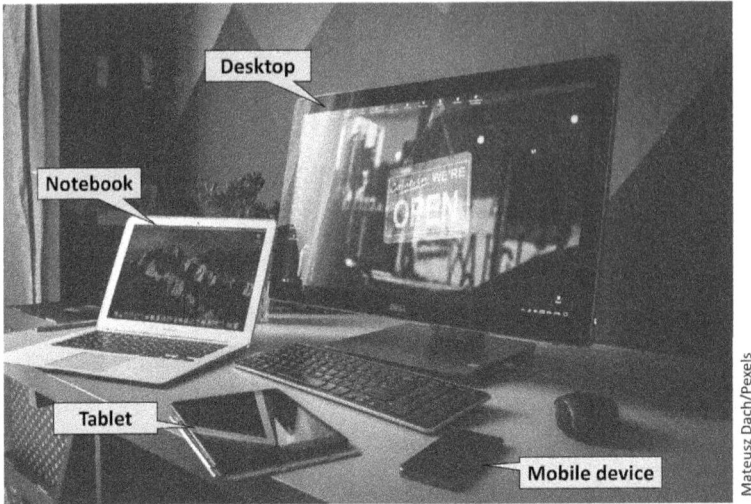

Figure 2.7 Personal computers include desktops, notebooks, and mobile devices

Source: Mateusz Dach/Pexels

A desktop computer is designed to be placed on a desk and is composed basically of a computer case, monitor, keyboard, and mouse. A notebook or a laptop is smaller than a desktop computer, is battery-powered, portable, and small enough to sit on your lap. Tablet computers are handheld, more portable than notebooks or laptops, and use touch-screen for typing than a keyboard or mouse. Smartphones usually smaller than tablets are mobile phones having touch-screen interface and internet access, which can do a lot of things computers can do.

In your college or university, you can use a desktop computer in the Lab to follow the instruction in a practical class. At any point in the institution, you can get an internet connection through your mobile device. Also, from your laptop, you can consult scheduled classes, do homework, and submit assignments.

A computer system is composed of many electronic parts. However, a computer needs more than electronic components to work. It is a necessary integration between hardware and software. Do you know what hardware and software are? How they work together? In the next chapter, you will find the answers to these questions and much more.

Summary

- Almost everything played every day for any organization will include some use of computers
- A computer is a system that receives information from the input, processes that information, and returns the output as a result
- A computer is a machine that converts data into information
- Computers are getting smaller and less expensive every day
- Modern technology helps the firm to be more efficient
- Personal computers include desktops, notebooks, and mobile devices

Review Questions

1. What is the difference between data and information?
2. Exemplify and describe at least three different types of PC.
3. Who is the computer's father, and why?
4. Why are computers essential for people today?
5. How computer systems help companies to be more efficient?

Case Study: Great Deal Real State

Great Deal Real State (GDRS) is a small company for sales and lease of properties in a little town in the west of Canada. They are now so proud to have implemented a new web system. The new web portal allows anyone looking for property for sale or lease to browse GDRS stock.

The company decided to hire a new employee to work inputting data into the new web system. The requirements for the position include being able to work with computer systems, the Internet, Microsoft Office, social media, and excellent communication. The HR posted the job position in a job website and received two resumes from candidates.

The first candidate is Jhon, with a bachelor's degree in business administration. He is an avid computer user, spending hours chatting on Facebook with friends. His major was finance. However, he likes accounting, as well. Seeing himself as an expert on social media during his studies, he decided not to take courses related to computers. Those courses skipped include an introduction to computers, e-commerce, and managing information systems.

The second candidate is Ann, and her major when graduating for a bachelor's degree in business was marketing. She is not addicted to computers and social media, but she has an Instagram and Facebook profile. When studying, she was outstanding in courses related to communication. Even though not being so addicted to computers, she took courses related to technologies like the introduction to computers, managing information systems, e-commerce, and web development. She thought it is essential to be updated with trends and new technologies, also be more than a computer user. Therefore, she dedicated time preparing herself for a future professional opportunity.

Case Questions:

1. Do you think GDRS did well investing in new technology?
2. How will the new system help GDRS to be more efficient?
3. Which candidate do you think fits better for the job position? Why?

CHAPTER 3

IT Infrastructure: Hardware and Software

Learning Objectives
- Describe hardware
- Identify the main components of hardware
- Describe input and output devices
- Describe software
- Understand the most common operating systems
- Work with Windows 10
- Explore file management

In Chapter 2, you learned that almost everything played every day for any organization will include some use of computer systems. Nowadays, companies are looking for ways to automate any remaining manual process to get more efficiency.

You also learned what a computer is and how you can use it in your daily life. This chapter goes more deeply into the computer system understanding and finds the answer to the question: What hardware and software are, and how they work together?

Chapters 1 and 2 gave you the notation of the importance of computer systems for the companies. From the business side, it is crucial to have a robust and powerful information technology infrastructure. Therefore, it is necessary to know computer needs and understand its components. A comprehension of hardware and software will give the manager the right notion and base to support decision making related to computer systems acquisition, maintenance, or upgrade.

Describe Hardware

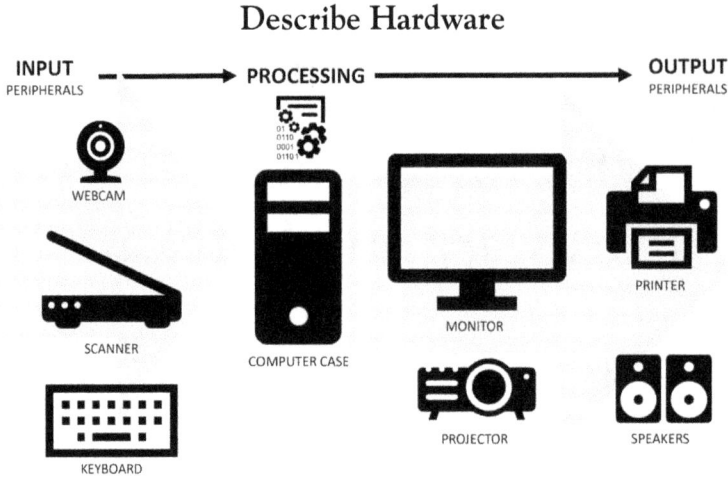

Figure 3.1 Computer and its peripheral devices

Source: Icon made by Pixel perfect from www.flaticon.com

The main tasks performed by computers are input, processing, output, and storage. A computer system needs different components to execute each of these tasks. The computer itself is the machine responsible for process data. However, it requires additional components called *peripheral devices* to perform the input, output, and storage functions (Figure 3.1). All these physical components, including the computer device itself, are hardware.

> According to Esteras, in a computer system, the *hardware* is any electronic or mechanical part you can see and touch (Esteras 2013).

Identify the Main Components of Hardware

Inside the computer case, that is, a metal or plastic box, you can find the main components of a computer system. There are the motherboard, central processing unit (CPU), and power supply. The motherboard is the main circuit board of an electronic device, and this board holds the CPU or microprocessor as well as other chips and circuits (Figure 3.2). The CPU is called the brain of the computer. The main reason relies on the fact that this microprocessor controls all function and processes all commands of a computer.

Figure 3.2 Motherboard and its CPU

Source: Pok Rie/Pexels

In 1971, Intel introduced the first microprocessor called Intel 4004. Nowadays, as explained by Moore's law, a microprocessor is smaller and powerful than its predecessors. Usually, about a 2-inch square, made of ceramic, covered by a heat sink, the microprocessor fits into the CPU socket located in the motherboard. Working in speed measured in megahertz (MHz) or gigahertz (GHz), the CPU selects instructions to be processed, performs arithmetic and logical comparisons, and stores the operation results in memory. This work at high speed is possible because a CPU is composed of several components. These components are the control unit (CU), arithmetic logic unit (ALU), floating-point unit (FPU), decode unit, cache memory, prefetch unit, registers, clock, bus, and instruction set. Figure 3.3 shows a diagram illustrating how a CPU works.

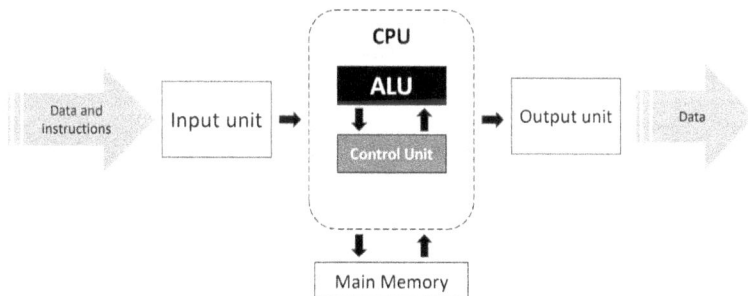

Figure 3.3 How the CPU works

Figure 3.3 shows the CPU receiving data and instructions from the input unit and organizing those in a fetching queue. Those instructions are processed, calculated, organized, and stored as part of the CPU processing work. Then, the resulting data are outputted through the output unit.

When a computer is turned on, it needs a set of data and instructions saved previously. These data and instructions stored in the read-only memory (ROM) begin the initial computer startup process. While in use or running, lots of tasks are performed by applications like games, word processors, Internet browsers, and so on. These processes need additional memory for execution, and this extra memory is called random-access memory (RAM).

ROM chips defined by the manufacturer are usually an integrated part of the computer motherboard. However, you can find expansion ports on the motherboard to replace or add RAM chips. The RAM chip capacity of storage is measured in gigabytes (GB).

If your computer is *slow,* before deciding to buy another one, maybe you could save some money just making an upgrade. Upgrading your computer means to replace the microprocessor with another one faster and add more RAM chips. It is a wise and economical way to extend the life of your computer.

A computer is an asset for companies and requires financial investment. Eventually, because of an increasing amount of data to be processed, the company needs more computer capacity. Working under a financial budget limit will require more from the manager about information technology investment. In this case, understanding how a computer is made of and how it works is very useful. In some situations, instead of replacing computers with new ones, the manager could consider the possibility of just upgrading microprocessors and RAM chips.

Describe Input and Output Devices

As learned, a computer is an electronic device developed to process data. There are too many things a computer can do and ease our life. However, to be an efficient tool for people needs, interactions are essential. This interaction means that people should have a way to enter data into computers and get back results from the processed data. It is the primary function of input and output devices. They serve as an interface between a human and machine. A keyboard is the most basic input device used to type and enter data into a computer. Also, the monitor is another primary output device used to show processed data to computer users. Go back to Figure 3.1 and take a look at some commons input and output devices.

A list of most common input devices would include the keyboard, webcam, mouse, scanner, microphone, joystick, and touchpad, to mention a few. On the other hand, the most common output devices would include the monitor, printer, projector, speakers, headphones, and others.

If you pay close attention, you will discover that all those devices have the objective to help us to communicate with computers. For this reason, they explore basic human senses like touch, sight, and hearing. The design and form are usually ergonomic to offer the most comfort possible for the users.

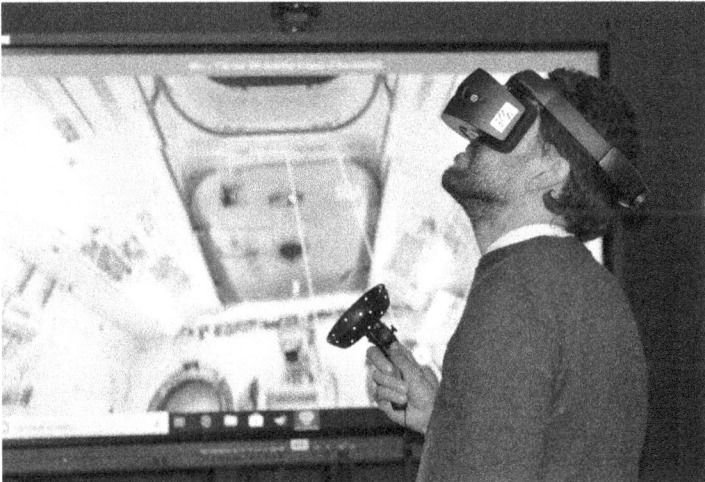

Figure 3.4 VR headset

Source: Laurens Derks/Unsplash

A virtual reality (VR) headset is a head-mounted device used to give the users an experience of artificial environments as being in the real world (Figure 3.4). It is an immersive experience. There are too many applications for VR like education, entertainment, medicine, architecture, military, and others.

Describe Software

Have you heard the term digital native before? This term does not refer to a particular generation, but an individual who was born in general after 1996 that marks the widespread adoption of digital technology. However, it does not means all children born today are digital natives. What defines a digital native is the interaction since early ages with technology.

We are living in an era of information and technology as part of our life. Computer systems are everywhere, and everybody at different levels is a computer user. However, computers are sophisticated devices, and in general, users do not understand how programs and utilities help computers run.

Those programs and utilities that help computers run are called software. In short, the software is a set of instructions telling hardware what to do and how to do it. Any program in your computer or apps on your smartphone is software. Games, Internet browsers, Microsoft Office, and Internet banking are examples of software.

There are different categories for software, depending on its purpose. The most common groups of software are operating systems, system utilities, and applications (Figure 3.5).

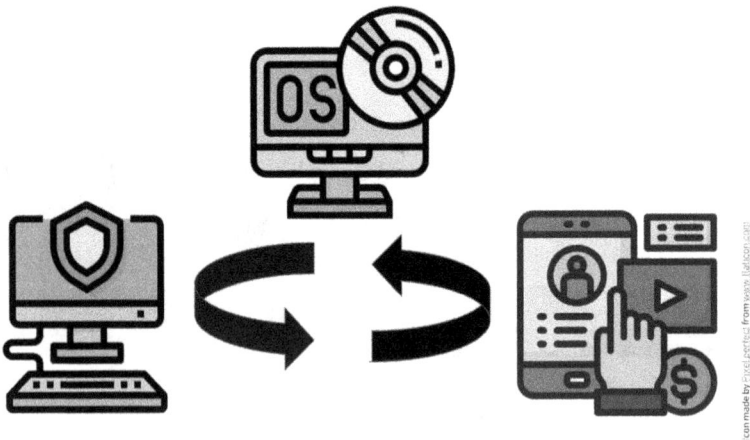

Figure 3.5 OS, system utilities and applications

Source: Icon made by Pixel perfect from www.flaticon.com

An operating system (OS) is an essential software responsible for managing and controlling all the programs on your computer device. This program provides the user interface to communicate with the hardware and other software on your computer. Also, it is the OS that controls all functions in your computer, like reading and writing data, memory allocation, program execution, error controls, and backup. How hard or easy will be the interaction with your computer will depend on a large part of the OS running.

System utilities are programs developed to help in the maintenance, repair, and protection of your computer. Some program utilities come with your OS. However, you can acquire and install additional system utilities on your computer. An antivirus program is an example of software utility frequently bought and installed additionally on computers.

Application software, application, or just app, is a group of software developed to help users with their most common daily tasks. This group of software includes a word processor, spreadsheet, business application, e-mail, media player, photo editor, Web browser, and much more. Microsoft Office is a suite that includes a list of different software applications used by companies. In this book, you will have the opportunity to learn how to work with the most used Microsoft Office applications.

Understand the Most Common Operating Systems

OS is the main program that defines how a computer device interacts with users, stores and manages files, runs different applications, manages memory, and lots of other functions. There are different OSes for different computers devices. Is your computer a PC, Mac, Tablet, or smartphone? Each of these computer devices comes with a specific OS. The most common OSes are Windows, macOS, Android, and Linux (Figure 3.6).

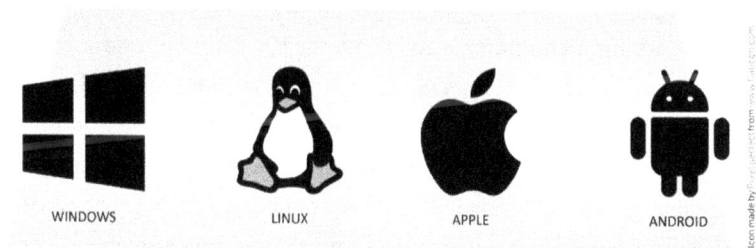

Figure 3.6 Most commons OSes

Source: Icon made by Pixel perfect from www.flaticon.com

Microsoft Windows is so far the most popular OS for PCs, residing on more than 95 percent OSes of the world's desktops. Windows 10 is the latest version of Microsoft OS, and it is possible to find a version for desktop, laptop, tablet, and smartphone. Because Microsoft Windows is a commercial software, some users prefer to have in their computer an open-source OS. This type of OS can be installed on a computer for free. The most popular open-source OS is Linux.

Developed by Apple, macOS X is the Macintosh operating system. It is an OS based on the Unix development language create to run on desktop and laptops manufactured by Apple. The company developed an intuitive and responsive mobile OS for its iPhone and iPad devices called iOS.

In terms of the number of users, Android is the most popular OS for smartphones and tablets. Developed by Google, Android has evolved continuously and has been installed in various devices from different manufacturers. Today, Android is a mobile OS standard for smartphones and tablets.

Work with Windows 10

If you are part of the 95 percent group of PC or desktop users around the world who have Microsoft OS, probably you are familiar with Windows 10. However, if you are part of the other group, probably macOS, or even if you just use your tablet or smartphone as a computer device being an Android user, you still may know about Windows 10. The reason is straightforward when you start to work in a company. The probability of you having to work on a computer with Microsoft OS like Windows 10 is very high.

To work on a computer with Windows 10, you will need a Microsoft account to log in to the OS through your account. Your Microsoft account includes a user name or e-mail and a password. Once you have logged in, you will see the desktop area or the main workspace for your computer (Figure 3.7). That is your start point to manage files, view e-mails, access the Internet, open applications, and much more.

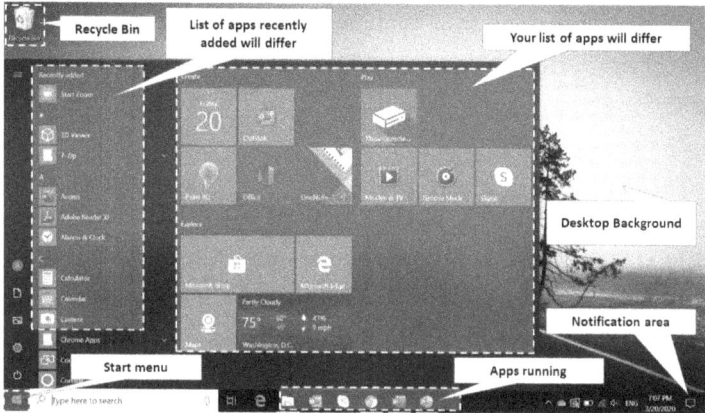

Figure 3.7 Windows 10 workspace

The Windows 10 workspace is dynamic. Its appearance will vary depending on how you use your desktop, installed applications, and personal configurations. However, there are some common elements to note. Your initial view usually is the big area named *Desktop background*, an icon on the left-top called *Recycle bin*, and a bottom-taskbar with a *Start* button menu at the bottom-left corner.

Click on the *Start menu* in the bottom-left corner of your screen to open programs, files, and settings. When you do that, a new window will open with areas where you can find files and applications. Those group areas could be *Most used*, *Recently added*, *Life at a glance*, *Create*, *Play*, and *Explore*.

When working with your Windows 10, you can find meaningful information on your bottom-bar like apps running, hour time, date, and notifications.

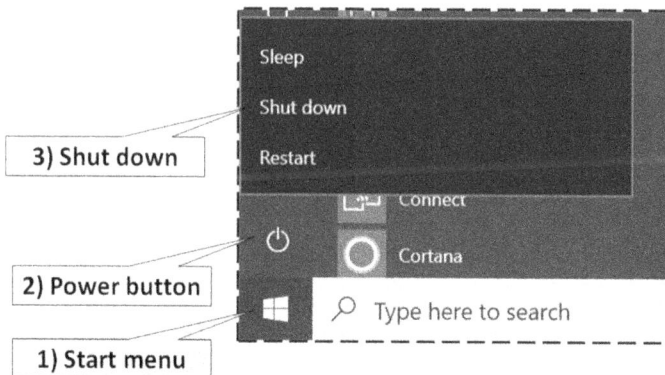

Figure 3.8 Windows 10 shutdown

Are you done using your computer? So, you can shut it down correctly (Figure 3.8). Just click on the *Start menu*, then choose *Power > Shut Down*.

Explore File Management

One of the most important things you can do when working with computers is file management. No matter what your position is in an organization, you also have to handle files. We can define the file as a digital collection of information stored on computers under a single name. Working with files means to create, open, close, save, name, delete, and organize them. The files can be organized into a folder structure that allows you to navigate through that structure. In Windows 10, the application called *File Explorer* is the program used to manage files and folders.

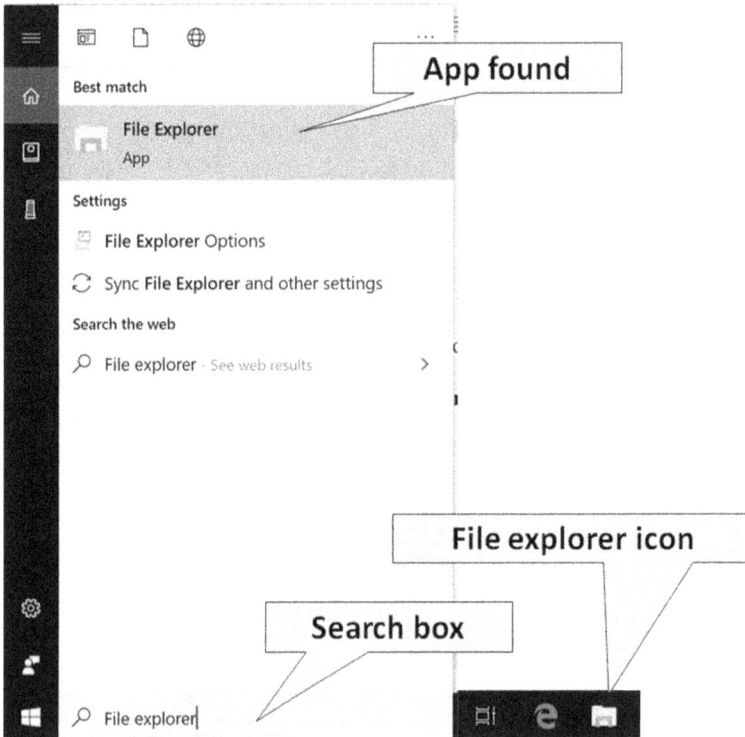

Figure 3.9 Opening File Explorer app

To open the File Explorer application, you can click on the *File Explorer icon* on the taskbar (Figure 3.9). Another way is just typing *File explorer* in the *Search box*. Once the app is found, just click on it to open the program.

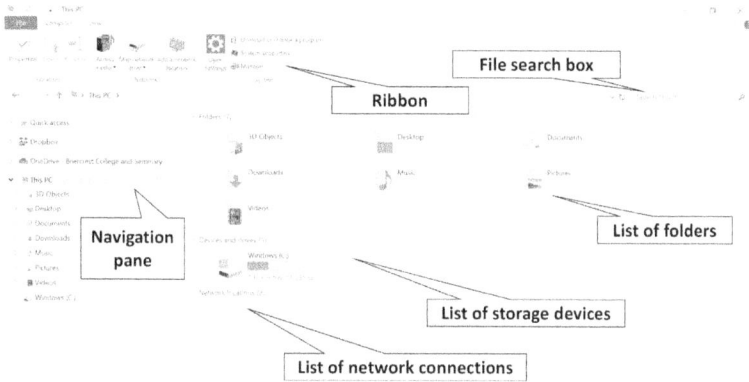

Figure 3.10 File Explorer

Use the *Navigation pane* to navigate between files, folders, drivers, and network. You can collapse and expand drivers and folders that include Quick access, OneDrive, This PC, and Network. Click on any of these items to list its contents on the right side. Also, you can use the *Search box* to find a file. When you select an item, the Ribbon will show the options related to the chosen object. Those options, depending on the selected item, can be properties, cut, copy, rename, delete, and so on.

Tech Article: Tips to Keep Your Computer Running Smoothly

Figure 3.11 Keep your computer running smoothly

Source: NewsUSA

(NewsUSA)—Buying a new computer's always a thrill—but sooner or later, your fast new machine will start to act like a clunker. Or will it?

With a few simple tips, you can keep your computer running smoothly. Sammsoft (www.sammsoft.com), a company that develops and publishes quality software products designed to secure, protect, maintain and enhance computer users' experience, provides the following tips:

1. Clean out your computer registry. Every Windows Operating System uses a registry or a central database that contains all of the settings for low-level operating system components, as well as any applications running on the platform. Every time you save something, run a new application or install or uninstall a program, new information is organized into your registry. But occasionally, the registry records something incorrectly. Over time, registry errors pile up and can start slowing down your computer. But running a registry cleaner, such as Advanced Registry Optimizer 2010 by Sammsoft, will fix registry errors and remove faulty files, helping your computer run quickly and smoothly.

2. Keep viruses under wraps. Run a virus checker regularly. If you have a high-speed wireless connection, don't use the Internet without a firewall. No antivirus strategy is perfect, so stay away from suspicious-looking Web sites and don't click on strange links in e-mails.

3. Get rid of unnecessary files. If you haven't used a program in months or years, delete it to reclaim valuable memory. But always back-up applications in case you want to reinstall them later, and don't delete applications that you don't recognize, as Windows might need them to run. Never remove WINDOWS or HOT FIX applications. Also, delete cookies and clear your Internet cache before you sign-off your computer.

4. Never turn off your computer before Windows has shut down. Doing so could harm the hard drive or result in lost data or Windows files.

5. Back up Your Computer. Hardware problems occur more than you might think, and you don't want to deal with the frustration of losing valuable data. Back up photos, Excel spreadsheets, Word documents—anything that you do not want to lose—on external hard drives or CDs.

For more information, visit www.sammsoft.com.

Summary

- Hardware is any electronic or mechanical part you can see and touch.
- Software is a set of instructions telling hardware what to do and how to do it.
- Application software is a group of programs developed to help users with their most common daily tasks.
- Microsoft Windows is so far the most popular OS for PCs.
- One of the most important things you can do when working with computers is file management.
- We can define the file as a digital collection of information stored on computers under a single name.

Review Questions

1. Explain how a computer works.
2. Define hardware and software.
3. What is the difference between RAM and ROM?
4. "A computer with more processing power can store more programs." Why is this statement not valid?

Windows 10 Project: Creating a New File

It is your first day at Mechanic Hills in the Parts department. Mrs. John, the parts manager, asked you to create an inventory of auto parts. Going to the stock, you found two bonnets, five bumpers, seven cowls, four wipers, and eight disk brakes. Using the File Explorer, you will create a new folder called intr2com into the Documents folder. After getting the new folder done, you will create a new file called *autoPartsList.txt* using the Notepad program.

Instructions

1. Open the *File Explorer*.
2. In the *Navigation pane*, select *This PC > Documents*.
3. With the folder Documents selected, go to the *Ribbon* and click on the option *New folder*.
4. Type *intro2com* for the folder name and press *Enter* on your keyboard.
5. With the new folder selected, go to the *Ribbon* and click on the option *Open*.
6. On the *taskbar*, type *Notepad* in the *Search box*.
7. Click on the *Notepad app*.
8. Type the auto parts list into the Notepad.
9. On the menu, select *File > Save*.
10. On the pop-up window, go to the Navigation pane and find the folder *intro2comp* (Figure 3.12).

11. Type *autoPartsList.txt* for the *File name.*

12. Click on the *Save button.*

13. Close the Notepad program.

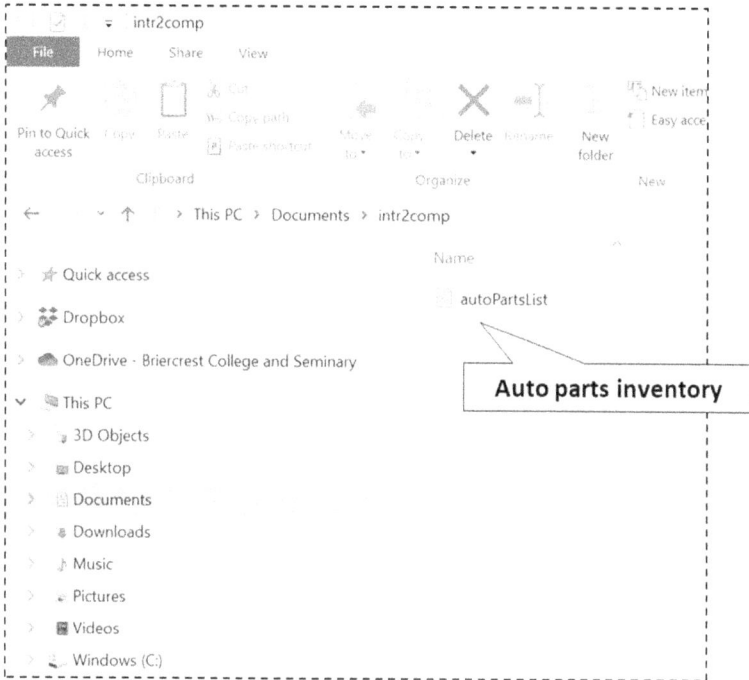

Figure 3.12 Auto parts inventory file created here

CHAPTER 4

Network, Internet, and Cloud Computing

Learning Objectives
- Understand computer networks
- Recognize the importance of the Internet
- Discuss cloud computing
- Send and receive e-mail using Gmail
- Store and share file with Google Drive
- Create a LinkedIn account

We live in the information age, in a globalized world, and networked society (Castells 2005). Local events are monitored worldwide in real time. This characteristic changes the social and economic behavior.

Networking within the context of computer systems can be approached from the hardware infrastructure point of view. Also, discussing the relationships built in a network structure is another approach. The latter refers to the possibilities that are made from the physical structure that is established in a network. In this case, we are talking about interaction, sharing, and collaboration.

In this way, a study on computer networks must address not only their physical structure but also the social relationships that are built from this structure. In a company, from a business point of view, both aspects are essential. Because they deal with financial issues related to infrastructure and investment, they also address issues related to efficiency, productivity, and profit. Companies in a competitive environment need to be dynamic, agile, productive, efficient, and profitable to survive.

This organizational scenario is naturally of interest to the professional who will work in this context. Becoming part of an organization that is dynamic, this professional is part of a network in an organic structure. No matter if this professional is working in an operational, management or strategic position. Therefore, this understanding of the environment that surrounds you must be part of your academic training and, consequently, professional.

In previous chapters, we learned about the importance of computing today. We discussed how to describe computers and how they work. We also learned about the difference between hardware and software and how they work analogously.

In this chapter, we will discuss network, Internet, and cloud computing. These are topics related to the structure of information technology. This network structure allows the interconnection of computer systems to increase and enhance the activities of organizations.

The importance and influence of social networks today are indisputable. Social media and social networks became possible, thanks to the advent of computer networks, both local and global. Therefore, it is an extremely relevant knowledge in computer learning.

Understand a Computer Network

In the not too distant past, when the concept of a network system was not yet widely used in companies, it is not difficult to imagine how problematic this would be. Each department had a computer. In general, one computer for human resources, another for sales, operations, finance, accounting, and so on. Thus, the information was centralized in each department, which needed to deal with the security of its data individually. The finance department continuously required to request information about sales, which were not available in real time. This information indeed passed between departments manually through some type of media, such as floppy disks, to copy data from one place to another. There was undoubtedly a need for additional work related to the processing of these data on a daily, weekly, monthly basis, and so on. As well as there was a need for processes to consolidate this information. Life was hard.

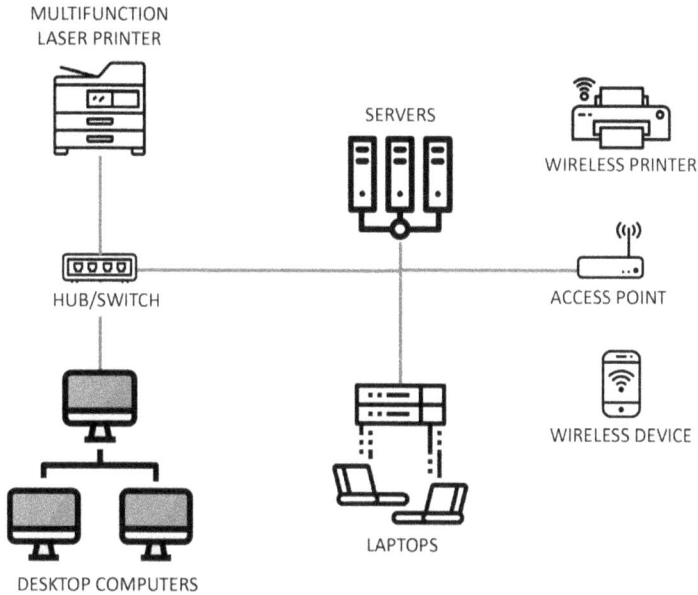

Figure 4.1 Computer network

Source: Icon made by Pixel perfect from www.flaticon.com

A computer network is a structure composed of hardware and software that allows communication and information sharing between two or more computer devices through a communication system (Figure 4.1). This communication system is the model that describes how networks are interconnected and the rules that organize the traffic of information.

Characteristics of a computer network are:

- Share resources from one computer to another
- Create files and store them on one computer, accessing the data from the other equipment connected to the network
- Connect a printer, scanner, or fax machine to a computer within the network structure and allow other computers to use the devices available on the network system

The networks can be classified according to their geographic scope. Thus, the classification of networks into local—LAN (local area network), metropolitan—MAN (metropolitan area network), and geographically distributed—WAN (wide area networks) is agreed.

The function of a LAN is to connect several computers and devices physically and also to a server (Figure 4.1). A server is a computer prepared to run 24 hours. In a LAN network, computers are connected through a bridge. Switches are bridge devices used to link the equipment that makes up a network. A network can be wired, wireless, or mixed. In a wired network, the connection between the computer and the switch takes place through cables (Figure 4.2).

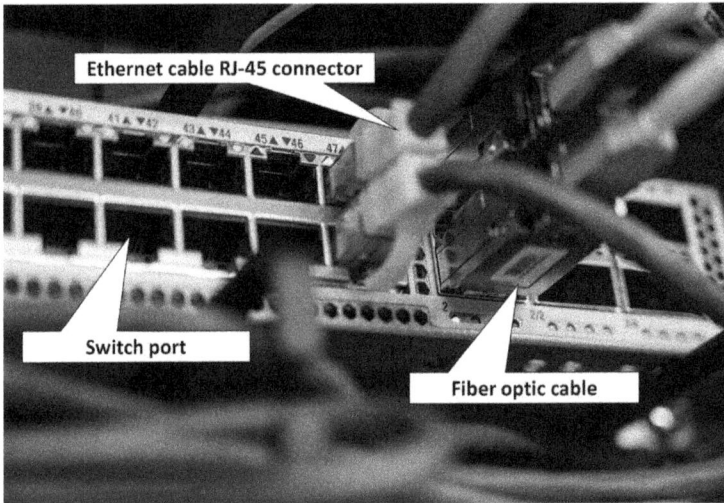

Figure 4.2 Switch network

Source: Brett Sayles/Pexels

The communication medium determines the speed at which data travels on the network. Wireless connections usually reach data rate speeds up to 300 megabits per second (Mbps). An ethernet cable offers speeds up to 100 Mbps, and fiber optic cable speeds up to 10 gigabytes per second (Gbps).

An interface is needed to connect a computer to a network structure, usually a network card. This network card is plugged into the motherboard, thus extending the functionality of the computer. Some motherboards already come as the network resource on the motherboard itself, which is called onboard. In the case of a wireless network, it is possible to plug a network adapter into the universal serial bus (USB) port.

In a network structure, data can travel from one device computer to another following a communication protocol called Transmission Control

Protocol/Internet Protocol (TCP/IP). Each equipment connected to the network receives an IP address so that the network system can identify the source and destination of the data. So, this data is broken into small packets to travel on the network structure. When the packets reach its destination, they are reassembled on the recipient computer.

IP address: 10.0.1.10   IP address: 10.0.1.20

Figure 4.3 Network packet traffic

Figure 4.3 shows how a Word document can be sent from computer A to computer B. The Word document is broken into packets, and the packets travel through the network to their destination. The source and destination of the packets are based on the IP address. TCP/IP determines the rules for how these packets should be created as well as the rules for sending and receiving.

As seen, data travels over the network in the form of digital packets. Could these packages be intercepted by someone with malicious intent? Yes, and it is what hackers do. They seek to invade systems and networks to collect privileged information for shady purposes. A hacker can use a sniffer, which is a software that monitors and analyzes traffic within a network. There are packet sniffers, Wi-Fi, networks and IP, among others. They usually use this type of software to try to discover valuable information, especially passwords.

Recognize the Importance of the Internet

The Internet was conceived as a military project of the U.S. government that had as its purpose the decentralization of information. It emerged as ARPANET in the 1960s. Over time, this project was released to universities for study and research. This project was then improved with the inclusion of the IP for data communication, the World Wide Web (WWW) that designates the hypermedia document system, and Hyper-Text Transfer Protocol Secure (HTTPS) for sending encrypted data, and others.

Figure 4.4 Tim Berners-Lee the World Wide Web inventor

Source: ©1994 CERN

The term INTERNET was first used in 1974 as an abbreviation for the provisional term internetworking. Later, in the 1980s, scientist Tim Berners-Lee (Figure 4.4) developed the WWW and created the first hypertext documents interconnected in information systems, accessible from any point of that primitive network. He was also the creator of HTML, a markup language used in the creation of websites, and HTTP, the primary protocol that establishes Internet connections worldwide. He developed the first Internet browser, *WWW*, in 1990. In the late 1990s, Tim Berners-Lee launched the first website.

Since then, the history of humanity would no longer be the same. A new revolution has started, the Internet revolution. Society has since been transformed, affecting the way people began to consume information, culture, services, products, entertainment, and knowledge. The Internet has become a milestone in the history of humanity, overcoming barriers by bringing people, cultures, worlds, and information together.

In the beginning, few could imagine its reach and influence in society today. Just for comparison, radio took 38 years to reach an audience of 50 million people, TV 13 years to achieve the same audience, the Internet only four years. Today, there are more than four billion active users around the world. Social networks appear, changing the way people relate. People have discovered on the Internet not only new ways of communicating but also of doing business. With the advent of the Internet, the way of doing trade, exchanging, selling, and buying goods has changed. It became more accessible and made possible the emergence of several electronic businesses, and e-commerce appeared.

Now that you know about the evolution and importance of the Internet, you may ask yourself: How does it work? The Internet is a worldwide computer network. These computers connected to the Web are called clients and servers. In this way, the entire Internet communication system works through requests and responses. The computer where the browser is installed, such as your computer, is the client. When you type the address of a webpage, browser requests the server where the page is stored. The server then processes this request and sends the requested page, which is then loaded into the browser of the computer that made the request.

As we have already seen, computers on a network are identified by their IP address. A webpage is stored on a computer that has the IP address, so to request the page, we should type the IP address where it is located. However, typing an IP address to open a webpage is not friendly. So, there are Domain Name Servers (DNS) that associates names to these addresses. So, to open the webpage of your educational institution, you do not need to know the IP address, just enter the Web address as *yourcollege.edu*. The DNS server is responsible for directing your request to the corresponding server where the page is stored.

Discuss Cloud Computing

Disruptive technology refers to a type of technological innovation that significantly changes how consumers, industries, or businesses operate. It also creates opportunities for the emergence of new kinds of business. The

Internet can undoubtedly be considered a type of disruptive technology that has significantly changed the behavior of consumers and the industry.

Cloud computing emerges as a new type of business that is made possible, thanks to the Internet. What is cloud computing? It is a technology that uses large-scale Internet connectivity to deliver computing as a service rather than a product (Figure 4.5). In this way, shared resources, software, and information are provided, allowing access through any computer, tablet, or cellphone connected to the Internet (*the cloud*).

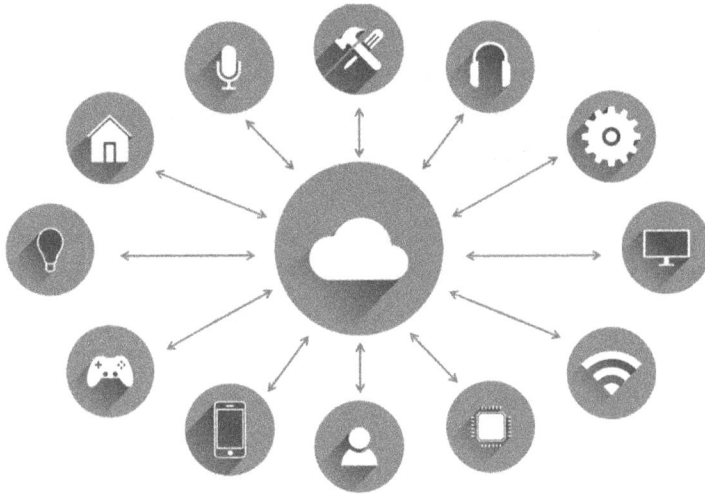

Figure 4.5 Cloud computing

Source: Tumisu/Pixabay

In cloud computing, the concept of client/server is widely used. In this case, you only need a device with Internet access to use any service available in the cloud. OneDrive, Microsoft Office 365, and Google Docs are examples of cloud computing, where users can store, share, create, and edit documents online. To use one of these services, simply open your Internet browser and access the address of the chosen services.

In a typical scenario without cloud computing, a company needs to invest in IT infrastructure. This investment includes the acquisition and maintenance of computers, installation of network infrastructure, purchase of software licenses, and hiring of technical staff to manage this infrastructure. With cloud computing, the company only subscribes to the services it needs to use and pays for the use. In this way, all costs related to infrastructure acquisition and maintenance are eliminated. On the other hand, the company needs to invest in a quality connection to the Internet.

Although cloud computing is a good option for many companies, it may not apply to all companies. It is necessary to take into account the implications related to storing all company information on a third-party server. It may have consequences for privacy and information protection policies. Another issue to consider is the ease or difficulty of migrating to another service provider because the supplier company no longer meets the company's needs. How difficult would it be to migrate your solution from Amazon Web Services (AWS) to Microsoft Azure or something else?

Cloud computing offers a wide variety of services, tools, and features to meet the needs of businesses. Among them, we can highlight at least the three main ones:

- **SaaS (Software as a Service)**: That allows access to the software without the need to purchase a license. In this case, the company can provide access to the software for its employees without the need to worry about installation, configuration, licensing, and updating. Enterprise resource planning (ERP), customer relationship management (CRM), and supply chain management (SCM) solutions are the most common.
- **PaaS (Platform as a service):** This solution is aimed at companies with software development teams. In this case, the entire on-demand development environment is contracted, in which it is possible to create, modify, and optimize software and applications in the cloud. The company that hires this service is only concerned with managing and maintaining its development team.
- **IaaS (Infrastructure as a Service):** In this case, the company can rent infrastructure resources, such as servers, routers, racks, data centers, hardware, and other tools that allow the transmission and storage of data. Thus, all investment in acquisition and maintenance is made by the company providing the service. The company that contracts this service can increase or reduce the usage according to the demand.

Send and Receive E-mail Using Gmail

An e-mail (electronic mail) is a method that allows you to compose, send, and receive messages through electronic communication systems. Some advantages of e-mail are productivity, easy access and management, privacy, communication with multiples people, and accessibility anywhere at any time. To use an e-mail service, you will need an *e-mail account* and an *e-mail address*. A typical e-mail address is composed of a username plus the symbol @ (at) plus the e-mail server domain provider. Example: *lawrence.page@gmail.com*.

Gmail is a free webmail service created by Google in 2004. This webmail service is an example of cloud computing and also has a paid option for business. To use the Gmail service, you have to sign up for Gmail (create a Google account). You can do that following these steps:

1. Go to the Google Account creation page on the link: *https://accounts. google.com/SignUp*.
2. Follow the steps on the screen to set up your account (Figure 4.6).
3. Sign in to Gmail using your account created.

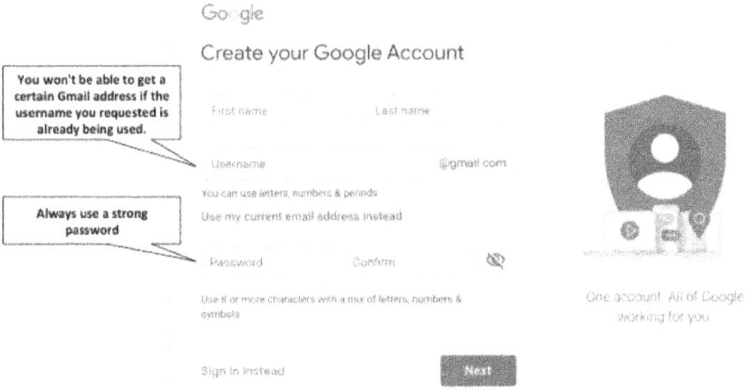

Figure 4.6 Google account creation page

Once you have a Gmail account, you can sign in to Gmail:

1. On your computer device go to *https://gmail.com.*
2. Enter your Google account e-mail and password (Figure 4.7).

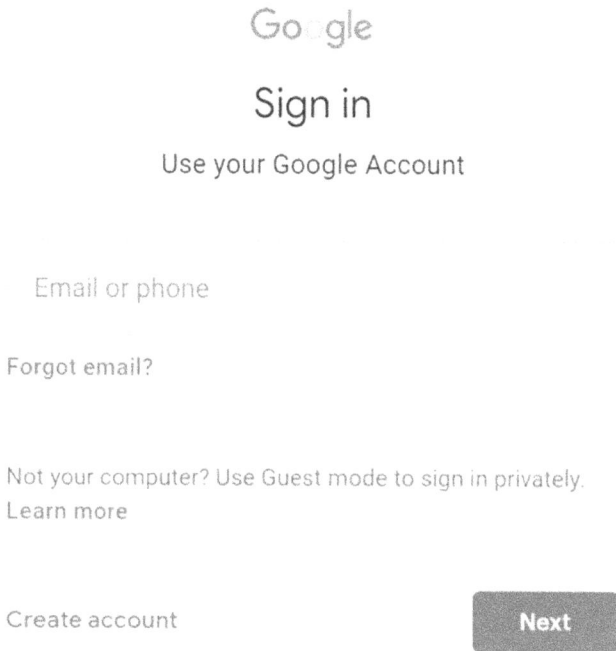

Go gle

Sign in

Use your Google Account

Email or phone

Forgot email?

Not your computer? Use Guest mode to sign in privately.
Learn more

Create account   Next

Figure 4.7 Google account creation page

To create a new Gmail message (e-mail), from the open Gmail inbox, click the *Compose* button in the upper left of the screen (Figure 4.8).

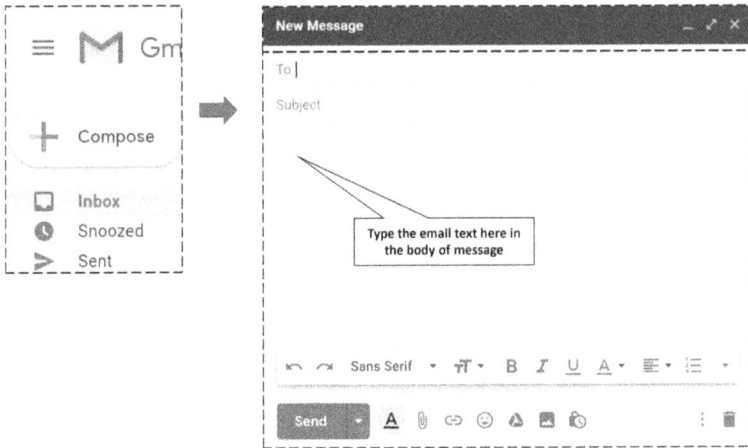

Figure 4.8 New message form

On the New Message form, fill out the *To* field, the *Subject* field, and the *body* of the message. Review the fields filled, and if everything is okay, click on the *Send* button. Your e-mail will be delivered to the recipient.

When communicating by e-mail, it is essential to keep in mind to be careful. Make use of *Netiquette*, which is the set of good manners and general rules of common sense that provide the use of the Internet in a more friendly, efficient, and pleasant way. Some states to have in mind include:

- Always identify yourself
- Do not assume you are on a first-name basis with the person you are e-mailing
- Cut the informal language
- Include a short subject line
- Mind your manners
- Avoid using all capital letters, this is perceived as SHOUTING
- Never spam others

Store and Share a File with Google Drive

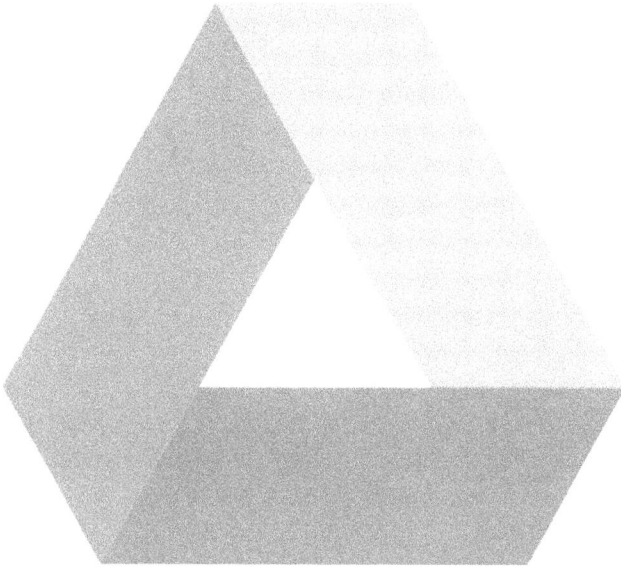

Figure 4.9 Google Drive logo

Source: Icon made by Pixel perfect from www.flaticon.com

Google Drive is a cloud storage and synchronization service, which also includes a set of online office applications that are comparable to Microsoft Office. These applications are the Google Docs Word processor, the Google Sheet spreadsheet, and the Google Slides presentation application. They are compatible with Microsoft Office, so it is possible to export and import Microsoft Office files. It is also possible to work together with colleagues by editing the same document simultaneously. If you have an assignment at your college to be written in a group, it can be shared and edited by everyone. The same applies to a company where a group of employees need to work on the same spreadsheet or report.

With your Google account created in the previous section, you receive a free space of 15 GB of storage. You can also use Google Drive apps for free. If you need more space, you can upgrade your free plan to a paid one and get more resources. For the business level, there is Google

Drive Enterprise, which, in addition to the applications mentioned, also includes other security and integration features.

The process of sharing files through Google Drive is relatively simple. The first step is to open Google Drive through the link *https://drive.google. com* and understand the options available (Figure 4.10).

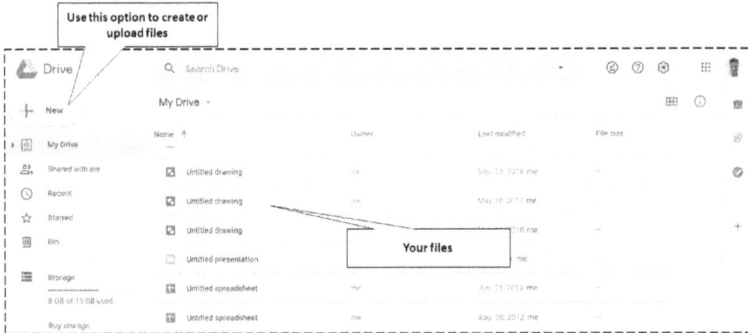

Figure 4.10 My Drive

When you access Google Drive, you will have access to the main application screen (*My Drive*). The main elements of this screen are the *New* button, *Search Drive* box, and the file area. When you want to create a new file or upload existing files on your computer to Google Drive, use the *New* button. When you have a considerable amount of files, just use the *Search Drive* box to find a file. To select a file, just click with the mouse button on the desired file.

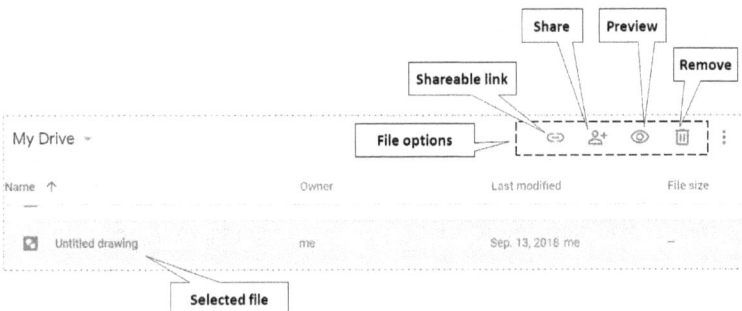

Figure 4.11 Selecting a file in the My Drive files area

When a file is selected, *Search Drive* will be replaced with a list of option icons (Figure 4.11). These icons in order from left to right are Shareable link, Share, Preview, and Remove. The icons for file sharing are *Shareable link* and *Share*. The *Preview* and *Remove* icons do what their description suggests.

A file can be shared in two ways, public and private. When a file is shared publicly, it means that anyone who accesses the share link will have access to the file. In the private form, only previously selected people will have access to the file.

To share publicly, click on the *Shareable link* icon. A window will open with the Web link to be shared. Copy and paste this link to share with others. By default, they will only be able to view your file when they access the link. To allow the file to be edited, click on *Sharing settings*. The *Share with others* window will be opened. In the first gray box, click to change *Anyone with the link can view* to ... *can edit* or ... *can comment*.

To share privately, click the *Share* icon. The *Share with others* window will open. Enter the e-mail addresses of the people you want to collaborate. *Can edit* is selected by default. But, you can change this option. To the right of the inbox and e-mails, click on the gray box to change from *can edit* to *can comment* or *can view*.

Create a LinkedIn Account

With the evolution of the Internet, people have discovered new ways to communicate and relate through the Web. One of these means of communication and relationship are social networks. A social network is a platform that aims to connect people and provide a means for them to share information between them, both personal and professional or commercial. Facebook, Twitter, Instagram, YouTube, and LinkedIn make up the list of social networks that are the most used at the moment.

Have you heard of LinkedIn? People, in general, are more used to social networks for personal use like Facebook and Instagram. LinkedIn is a social network developed for professional purposes, such as career and business. It is a social network that focuses on promoting the relationship of people interested in discussing career and work issues within a more formal and organized environment. As a result, it became a center for promotion, dissemination, and professional development. In some countries, it is the primary tool used by companies to advertise job vacancies and hire new professionals.

Having a profile on this platform is essential for your professional development and future placement in the job market. The most important thing is that you can have your profile and curriculum on the platform for free.

If you do not already have a LinkedIn account, the process for creating your account is relatively simple. Just access the link *https://www.linkedin.com* and click on the *Join* button (Figure 4.12). LinkedIn will guide you through the steps of adding information to your profile.

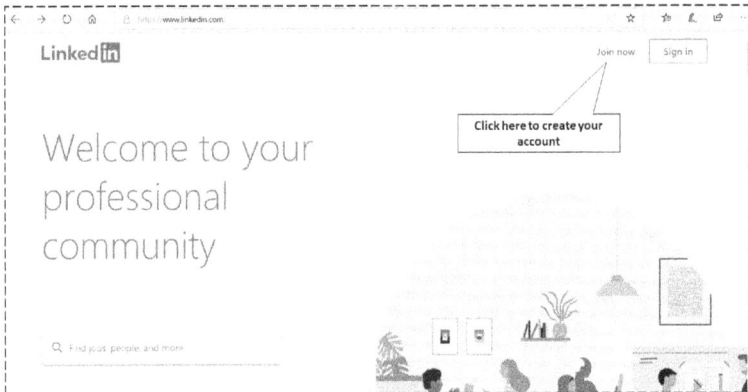

Figure 4.12 LinkedIn webpage

It is important to remember that your LinkedIn interactions can influence your career. So, be careful with postings, choose a suitable photo, leave the jokes aside, and do not send invitations in bulk and without criteria to strangers. Be professional.

Tech Article: Your Online Reputation: Handle With Care

Figure 4.13 Your online reputation

Source: NewsUSA

(NewsUSA)—Maintaining a positive reputation online is indispensable in today's digital age. It's time to take a long, honest look at how you manage your online reputation.

Consider these statistics:

According to 2011 Cone Online Influence Trend Tracker survey, 87 percent of consumers said positive information they've read online reinforced their decision to purchase a recommended product or service. (This figure 4.13 is up from 67 percent in 2010.) The 2010 Microsoft Cross-Tab survey found similar results, with 85 percent of recruiters and human resources professionals saying that a positive online reputation influences their decision-making.

With something as fragile as a reputation, how do you begin to protect it? After all, just one bad Facebook photo, and you may not get a call for an interview. Just one bad review or news article, and your company loses phone calls and customers.

"We don't have a lot of control about what others say about us, but we have a lot of control about what we say about ourselves and our company," says Todd William, CEO of Reputation Rhino, an online reputation management company in New York. "I strongly encourage individuals and companies to actively engage in social media, blogging and proactive public relations like press releases, networking and charitable activities."

- Don't know where to start? Here's a list:
- Google your name to see where you stand.
- Create a complete profile on popular social media sites like Facebook, Twitter and LinkedIn.
- Participate actively in online communities.
- Publish positive reviews of satisfied clients or customers.
- Monitor social media mentions for your name or business.
- Update your blog regularly.
- Use SEO (search engine optimization) to make sure positive content comes up first for your name or business.

Unfortunately, reputation management can be a great deal of work and worry. Do you have the time or necessary expertise?

If you answered "No" to this question, don't fret. Today's businesses and busy professionals are turning to online reputation management companies.

"Online reputation management is the art and science of creating a positive first impression when someone is looking for you or your company online," says William. "Online reputation management can remove or suppress negative search results, optimize positive online content, outrank complaint and review sites and fight libel and online defamation."

For more information, visit www.reputationrhino.com.

Summary

- A computer network is a structure composed of hardware and software that allows communication and information sharing between two or more computer devices through a communication system.
- The Internet has become a milestone in the history of humanity, overcoming barriers by bringing people, cultures, worlds, and information together.
- Cloud computing is a technology that uses large-scale Internet connectivity to deliver computing as a service rather than a product.
- Gmail is a free webmail service created by Google in 2004, and this is an example of cloud computing.
- Google Drive is a cloud storage and synchronization service.
- LinkedIn is a social network developed for professional purposes, such as career and business.

Review Questions

1. What is the importance of network systems for business?
2. How does the Internet work?
3. How can social networks improve the business?
4. Why should you have a LinkedIn profile?

Case Study: No Internet, No Network, No Business

The Internet is the number one way for any business to have any sort of value for customers and clients alike, especially in times where they are not capable of coming to you. Or, they may not want to go to you, preferring to do their shopping, question asking, problem searching, work, studies, and or business proposals from a phone or laptop while leaving the socializing to a night out with some friends.

Throughout an entire couple of weeks or so they are not walking into your door, you are at least missing out on a golden opportunity to observe a potential customer's needs, wants, and buying habits. It may often be flat out impossible, even to create marketing strategies without this information that your competitors probably already have. It may also be impossible to advertise yourself, your product, or so much as a network without it.

The Internet has made it easier than ever to gain allies on the road to success necessarily. Back then, almost everything was mostly neighbor-based, meaning whoever was not on the same block probably did not exist in your business world, at least not directly. When a network between groups is established, think about all the information and ideas that can immediately be pooled in, information and ideas that might make you more noticeable.

More noticeability equals more opportunities. Maybe a relationship with another company or individual client could help you expand and reach a larger bank of consumers. Perhaps doing so on your own would have been more expensive and potentially bankrupting. After all, a good 7 out of 10 businesses fail within the first 10 years. And, without the ability to futureproof themselves through the use of the Internet and networking, anyone could fail as quickly as overnight, businesses being no exception.

Case Questions

1. What is the role of network and Internet for companies?
2. How the Internet help companies improve the business?
3. List the pros and cons of being connected.

CHAPTER 5

Making Business Easy: The Microsoft Office 2019

Learning Objectives
- Explore Microsoft Office 2019
- Create documents with Microsoft Word
- Create worksheet and chart with Microsoft Excel
- Create a presentation with Microsoft PowerPoint

Since the beginning of computer history, companies realized the importance of this equipment as a powerful tool for business. In the beginning, only large corporations had access to this technology. But, over the years, as demonstrated by Moore's law, computers have become more efficient and affordable. Therefore, even micro and small companies can benefit from their resources.

Since its founding, Microsoft has also realized this and created a solution for business. This software solution is a suite of programs called Microsoft Office. The line of office packages for computers has followed users' routines since the beginning of the Windows launch. Among the most diverse competitors, Microsoft Office has always stood out as a complete, robust, easy-to-learn and user-friendly tool.

When operating a business, you know all of the different tasks that have to go into it. You will be doing everything from mailing out correspondence to conducting presentations. When working with Microsoft Office 2019 in your company, you will find that the tasks not only become more manageable, but things are getting done more efficiently.

When a company decides to switch to Microsoft Office 2019, it will notice even the most daunting tasks that need to be completed in your business suddenly become easy the moment that you put the program into effect.

Microsoft Office 2019 has improved all-around quality. Although you can use the application for personal everyday use and even school, you will be amazed at how it will make your business dealings run much more smoothly. This application can be incorporated into every aspect of a company at every level. So, whether you want to construct a contract or create a financial report, Microsoft Office 2019 is more than qualified to complete the task. This suite also will provide all resources a business needs to achieve productivity and team working.

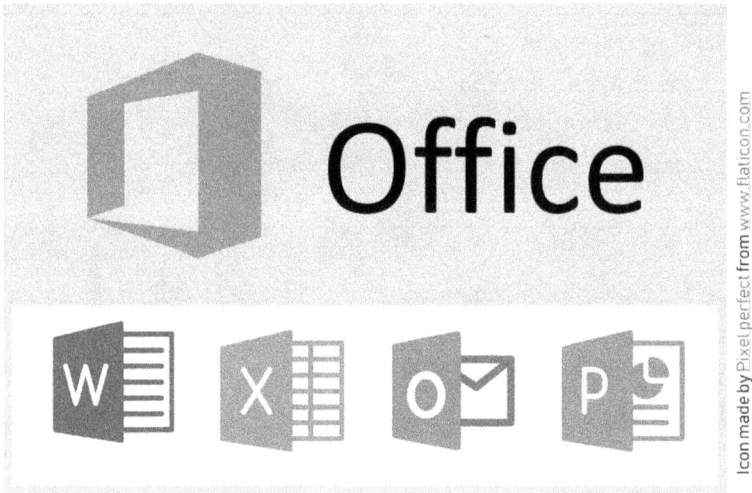

Figure 5.1 *Microsoft Office*

Source: Icon made by Pixel perfect from www.flaticon.com

The Microsoft Office suite since its launch has been adopted by the vast majority of companies worldwide, which has given it total popularity. Despite the alternatives, this suite has become a standard for a wide variety of organizations. Whether because of its functions, stability, or because it is entirely intuitive, the truth is that the general public has already become accustomed to this powerful tool.

The fact that it is a tool adopted by most companies gives advantages to those who know how to use it. That is, all the functions and skills we acquire in the software are immediately transferable to new jobs and companies. This aspect is the advantage of portability.

Communication is also another essential factor. It is effortless to communicate and collaborate more effectively with Microsoft Office tools, whether with Outlook for e-mail, Excel spreadsheets, Word, and PowerPoint features (Figure 5.1). As the vast majority of professionals are aware of these tools, communication and information sharing become easier.

This facility is not restricted to the fact that Microsoft Office is a standard today in most companies. Microsoft solutions are characterized by being friendly and easy to use. It does not mean that they are limited. On the contrary, they are powerful tools. This combination makes it a tool that helps organizations to become more productive. Yes, the productivity you get from using Microsoft Office is another significant factor.

Although, in this chapter, we are referring to Microsoft Office 2019, the content applies in the same way to Microsoft Office 365. What is the difference between them? The difference relates to the form of purchase or license to use the solution. Microsoft Office 2019 is sold as a one-time purchase, which means you pay a one-time upfront cost to get Microsoft Office 2019 applications for a computer. Microsoft Office 365 is a subscription service that ensures you always have the latest modern productivity tools from Microsoft. Therefore, the difference between the two does not refer to the functionalities, but the form of acquisition.

Tech Article: 5 Free Ways to Work and Collaborate

NewsUSA

Figure 5.2 Software like Skype and Join.me make it easy to collaborate

Source: NewsUSA

(NewsUSA)—You don't have to be a tech geek to work smarter in and out of the office; there are some straightforward, free software programs that will help you connect with colleagues for conversation and collaboration.

Let technology simplify your work life with these free software programs. Each offers the ability to get work done on your own time and from anywhere.

- Skype. Sign up for a free Skype account, then send instant messages or make calls from your computer. It helps if you have a microphone and video camera connected to your computer. Try it out at www.skype.com.
- join.me. This program lets you share your desktop. Once you sign up for the free account, you can send up to 250 colleagues to http://join.me. After they enter the nine-digit code that you provide, they can see your desktop and files. This is great for meeting, training and group editing.
- Open Office. Build documents, spreadsheets and presentations without the expense or megabit-girth of Microsoft Office. Download Open Office onto your computer, and use the free suite of open-source software as if it were Office. It can save and open Office files, so no one will know the difference. More details are at http://openoffice.org.
- Google Docs. Google Docs allows you to host documents for free, so everyone can have a look. Go to http://docs.google.com to download your file, then share it as a link or send an e-mail to collaborators. You can change the settings to allow users to edit the document (you can track changes) or limit them to viewing only. You do not need to have Gmail, though you will need to create a free Google account.
- Tungle.me. Among Microsoft Outlook, Google Calendar and iCal, you might have trouble sorting through your date book. Tungle.me lets you sync these calendars and provides a place where people can schedule time with you—without your involvement. Go to http://tungle.me for more information.

Explore Microsoft Office 2019

Microsoft Office 2019 runs only on Windows 10 and Macs purchased from 2009. It has an integrated translator, so users of Word, Excel, and PowerPoint can translate texts directly in the document, without having to resort to the Web version of the service. Some other things that came with Office 2019 are:

- Microsoft Word, Excel, Access, Outlook, Publisher, and Skype
- Create PowerPoint presentations, reports, and data models
- Travel and delivery summary cards
- Creation of math equations with LaTeX equation in Word
- Focused inbox
- Word translator in Word, Excel, and PowerPoint.
- 1 TB of online file storage and sharing and much more!

The traditional Microsoft Office package came with Word, Excel, PowerPoint, and Outlook. But, Microsoft Office 2019 core comes with more applications by default.

In this chapter, you will learn the three main programs from the core of Microsoft Office 2019. You will learn how to create documents using Word, develop spreadsheets with Excel, and design presentations with PowerPoint.

Create Documents with Microsoft Word

Microsoft Word (or only Word) is a word processing program designed to help you create professional-quality documents. It is the most popular and widely used word processor in the world. Its interface is very user friendly and intuitive, with commands and functions easily accessible. With its document formatting tools, Word helps you organize and write your documents more efficiently. This application also includes advanced editing and proofing tools. Some of the Word features are:

- Copy and move text, paragraphs, drawings, and other objects with drag and drop
- Simplified graphics, spreadsheets, and pictures insertion
- Variety of font types and sizes, including graphic symbols
- Variety of templates for different types of documents
- Creating document styles and models with predefined formatting
- WYSIWYG (What You See Is What You Get) view
- Text highlights such as borders, shading
- Character highlighting
- Preview files
- Built-in spell checker
- Features such as headers, footers, multicolumn text, generator of indexes and indexes, and macro editor
- Tools for producing drawings and logos
- Editor of mathematical and scientific formulas
- Auto-formatting of texts and documents
- Resources for creating labels, model letters, envelopes, and catalogs

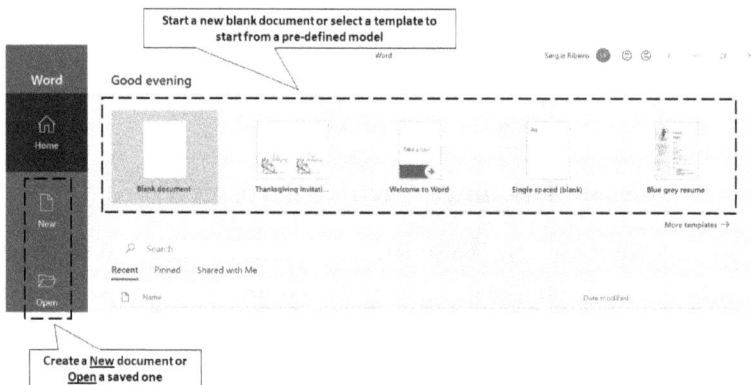

Figure 5.3 **Starting the Microsoft Word**

When you start the Word, your first step is to choose whether to start from a blank document, create your document from pre-existing templates, or just edit a previously saved document (Figure 5.3). From this point on, the process of editing and sharing documents occurs in the same way. The powerful editing and proofreading tools will help you work together to obtain the best final result in your text.

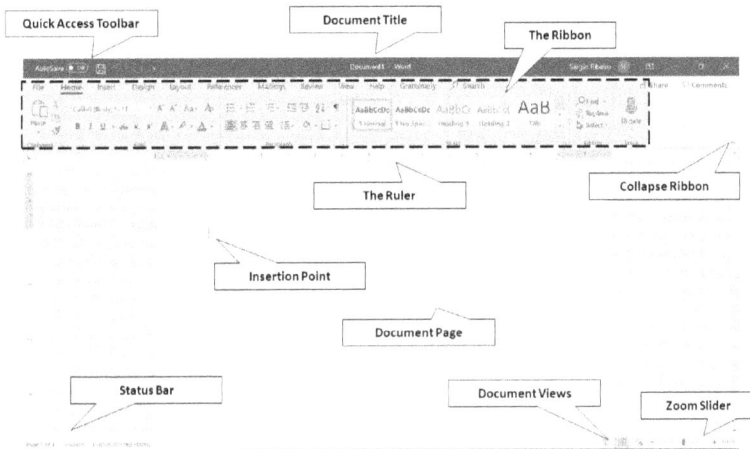

Figure 5.4 Word interface

When you open Word choosing to create a new document, choose a template, or access recently edited documents, you will see to Word interface (Figure 5.4). Some of the main elements on your Word interface are:

- **Quick Access Toolbar:** Lets you access common commands like the AutoSave button to turn it on or off, Save, Undo, Redo, and Customized Quick Access Toolbar.
- **Document Title:** Lets you know the document file filename. When you start a new document, your default filename will be Document1. However, after saving your document, the document title will change according to the document filename given.
- **Ribbon:** This is a user interface element located below the Quick Access Toolbar and the Title Bar. The Ribbon contains multiple tabs, each with several groups of commands like

Home, Insert, Design, Layout, References, Mailing, Review, View, and Help.

- **Collapse Ribbon:** This button lets you collapse the ribbon and get a more editing space area.
- **The Ruler:** There are two rulers located at the top and to the left of your document page. Both rulers help you to make alignment and spacing adjustments.
- **Insertion Point:** It is located in the upper-left corner of your document. The blinking insertion point indicates where you begin creating your text on the page.
- **Document Page:** This is the area where you will type and edit the text in the document. When you place your cursor on the document page, the cursor changes to a large *I*, which is called the *I-beam*. You can click on any part of your document page to move your insertion point there.
- **Status Bar:** Lets you know the number of current page, as well as how many pages your document has. Also, it informs you of the number of words in your document and used language.
- **Document Views:** This is used to change the way you see your document. You can change the document view to Read Mode, Print Layout, and Web Layout. The Read Mode displays your document in full-screen mode. The Print Layout is selected by default and shows the document as it would appear on the printed page. The Web Layout mode shows how your document would look like as a webpage.
- **Zoom Slider:** It is used to zoom-in and zoom-out your document page. You can click and drag the slider or just click on the "-" or the "+" buttons to change the zoom visualization.

Let's create a flyer to learn how to use the Word interface and its features.

Part 1: Create a New Document and Insert Text

1. *Start Word* and then click on the *Blank document* option.
2. In the *Ribbon,* click on the *Home tab*, find the *Paragraph group* and click on the *Show/Hide* ¶ button to display the nonprinting characters in the document.
3. Make sure your *insertion point* is at the beginning of the document page.
4. Type the following text pressing the **ENTER** key from your keyboard once after each paragraph.
   2020 SUPPORT STAFF FAIR—TORONTO EVENTS
   WE'RE
   HIRING
   DOWNTOWN
   999 MAIN STREET, ON
   HIRING FOR
   FOOD SERVICE
   MAINTENANCE & OPERATIONS
   TRANSPORTATION
   YOU MUST COMPLETE AN APPLICATION IN THE WEBSITE
   APPLY HERE
   WWW.TORONTOEVENTS.COM
   OR CALL FOR INTERVIEW AT
   (999) 999-9999
5. On the *Quick Access Toolbar*, click on the *Save* button and type *MyFirstFlyer* as the filename for your document.
6. Take a moment to review your document and study the Word interface based on Figure 5.5 to become familiar with the commands.

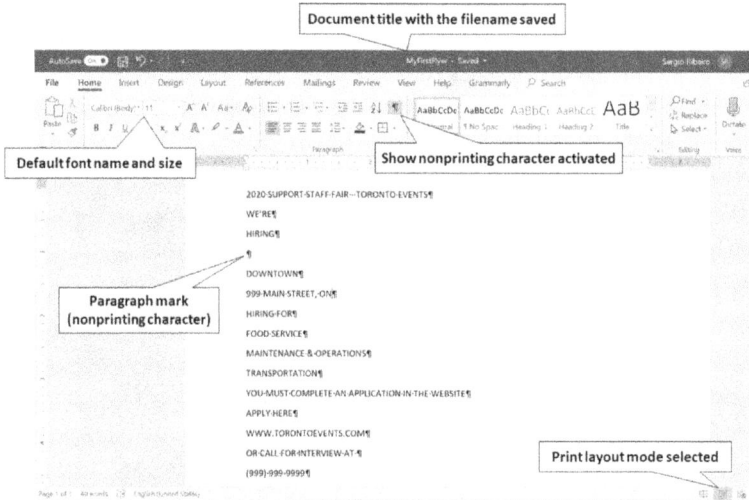

Figure 5.5 MyFirstFlyer document

Part 2: Formatting

1. Select the first paragraph of text: *2020 SUPPORT STAFF FAIR—TORONTO EVENTS*. Click on the *Home tab*, in the *Paragraph group*, click on *Borders* and select *Outside Borders*. Click on *Center*. Click on *Shading* and select *Blue, Accent 1, Dark 50%*. In the *Font group*, change the *font size* to *16*.

2. Select the second and third paragraphs of text: *WE'RE HIRING*. In the *Font group*, click on *Text Effects and Typography* and select *Blue, Accent color 1, Shadow*, change *Font Size* to *72*. Then, in the *Paragraph group*, click on *Center*. Click on *Line and Paragraph Spacing* and select *1.0*, then select *Remove Space After Paragraph*.

3. Select the fifth and sixth paragraphs of text: *DOWNTOWN 999 MAIN STREET, ON*. In the *Font group*, click on *Bold* and change the *font size* to *14*. In the *Paragraph group*, click on *Center*. Then, click on *Line and Paragraph Spacing* and select *1.0*, then select *Remove Space After Paragraph*.

4. Select only the paragraph of text: *999 MAIN STREET, ON*. In the *Paragraph group*, click on *Line and Paragraph Spacing* and select *Add Space After Paragraph*.

5. Select only the paragraph of text: *HIRING FOR*. In the *Paragraph group*, click on *Line and Paragraph Spacing* and choose *Add Space Before Paragraph*. In the *Font group*, click on *Text Effects and Typography* and select *Orange, Accent color 2, Outline*. Click on *Bold* and change the *font size* to *20*.

6. Select the paragraphs of text: *FOOD SERVICE MAINTENANCE & OPERATIONS TRANSPORTATION*. In the *Font group*, click *Bold* and change the *font size* to *14*. In the *Paragraph group*, click on *Bullets*.

7. Select the paragraph of text: *YOU MUST COMPLETE AN APPLICATION IN THE WEBSITE*. In the *Paragraph group*, click on *Borders* and select *Outside Borders*. Click on *Center*. Click on *Shading* and select *Black, Text 1*. In the *Font group*, change the *font size* to *16*.

8. Select the paragraph of text: *APPLY HERE*. In the *Paragraph group*, click on *Line and Paragraph Spacing* and choose *Add Space Before Paragraph*. In the *Font group*, click on *Text Effects and Typography* and select *Orange, Accent color 2, Outline*. Click on *Bold* and change the *font size* to *20*.

9. Select the paragraphs of text: *WWW.TORONTOEVENTS.COM OR CALL FOR INTERVIEW AT*. In the *Font group*, click *Bold* and change the *font size* to *14*.

10. Select the paragraph of text: *(999) 999-9999*. In the *Font group*, click *Bold* and change the *font size* to *24*.

11. On the *Quick Access Toolbar*, click on the *Save* button.

Part 3: Inserting Graphic Elements (shapes)

1. Go to line four (it is the line without text). Click on the *Insert tab*, in the *Illustrations group*, click on *Shapes* and select *Ribbon Tilted up*. Click on line four again to insert the shape there. With the object shape selected on the *Format tab*, in the *Arrange group*, click on *Wrap text* and select *In Line with Text*. In the *Size group*, change *Shape Width* to *6.5"* (inches). Point the mouse cursor over the select Shape and click on it with *right-mouse-button*. In the *menu options*, select *Add text*. This action will allow you to type a text inside the shape

form. *Type* inside the object form the text: *JULY 15, 2020*. Select the text typed, click on the *Home tab*, in the *Font group*, click on *Bold* and change the *size* to *26*.

2. Go to line seven (it is the line with the text *HIRING FOR*). Click on the *Insert tab*, in the *Illustrations group*, click on *Shapes* and select *Text Box*. Click on line seven again before the letter *H* of the word *HIRING* to insert the shape there. With the object shape selected on the *Format tab*, in the *Arrange group*, click on *Wrap text* and select *Square*. In the *Size group*, change *Shape Width* to *3"* (inches). In the *Text group*, click on *Align Text* and select *Middle*. In the *Shape Styles group*, choose *Colored Fill – Orange, Accent 2*. Inside the object shape, type the following text pressing the **ENTER** once after each paragraph.

INTERVIEW
9 AM TO 2 PM

3. Select the text typed, click on the *Home tab*, in the *Font group*, click on *Bold* and change the *size* to *26*. In the *Paragraph group*, click on *Center*. Then, click on *Line and Paragraph Spacing* and select *1.0*, then select *Remove Space After Paragraph*.

4. Go to line 12 (it is the line with the text *APPLY HERE*). Click on the *Insert tab,* in the *Illustrations group*, click on *Shapes* and select *Text Box*. Click on line 12 again before the letter *A* of the word *APPLY* to insert the shape there. With the object shape selected on the *Format tab*, in the *Arrange group*, click on *Wrap text* and select *Square*. In the *Size group*, change *Shape Width* to *3"* and *Shape Height* to *1.5"*. In the *Text group*, click on *Align Text* and select *Middle*. In the *Shape Styles group*, choose *Colored Fill – Green, Accent 6*. Inside the object shape, type the following text pressing the **ENTER** once after each paragraph.

REMEMBER TO BRING:
RESUME
SCHOOL DIPLOMA
PERTINENT CERTIFICATION

5. Select the text typed, click on the *Home tab*, in the *Font group*, click on *Bold* and change the *size* to *14*. In the *Paragraph group*, click on

Center. Then, click on *Line and Paragraph Spacing* and select *1.0,* then select *Remove Space After Paragraph.*

6. Select the paragraphs of text: *RESUME SCHOOL DIPLOMA PERTINENT CERTIFICATION.* In the *Paragraph group,* click on *Bullets.*

7. On the *Quick Access Toolbar,* click on the *Save* button.

Part 4: Preview and Printing the document

1. Press **Ctrl** + **Home** on your keyboard, the insertion point will be moved to the top of your document.

2. Click on the *File tab,* click on *Print* to display the *Print Preview.* Your completed document should look similar to Figure 5.6.

3. If you want to print your document, select any printer connected to your system and click on the *Print* button.

Figure 5.6 MyFirstFlyer document ended

Create Worksheet and Chart with Microsoft Excel

Microsoft Excel or only Excel is a spreadsheet editor. Through its various fields and columns, it is possible to make calculations, graphs, and many other mathematical and comparative constructions. It is a software that allows you to create tables, calculate, and analyze data. Excel was developed by Microsoft and has been widely used by companies for both commercial and private purposes for carrying out financial and accounting operations. Its most common applications include accounting, budgeting, financial control, sales, reporting, planning, to name a few.

Its new version in the Microsoft Office 2019 suite brings improvements such as new functions, new graphics, improved visual elements, improvements in accessibility features, new sharing features, improvements in pivot tables, Power BI integration, and Power Query.

Because of its extensive use by companies, its domain becomes essential for entering the job market. In careers such as accounting, finance, human resources, and marketing, a good knowledge of Excel becomes indispensable.

Before starting to use Excel, you need to familiarize yourself with some commonly used terms.

- **Workbook:** Is the Excel document composed of one or more pages called *worksheet* or *spreadsheet*.
- **Column:** A vertical group of cells in a worksheet. In Excel, each column is identified by a letter on the top of the spreadsheet—called *column heading*.
- **Row:** A horizontal group of cells in a worksheet. In Excel, each row is identified by a number on the left of the spreadsheet—called *row heading*.
- **Cell:** An intersection of a column and row. When you point to and click the cell, it is outlined and ready to accept data— the selected cell is called an *active cell*. The data or anything you type in a cell is called *cell content*. The intersecting column letter and row number (e.g., A1 or C10) is the *cell reference* or *cell address*.
- **Range:** A group of selected cells on a worksheet (adjacent or nonadjacent). A range of cells is referred to as A1:C3. The colon (:) between two cell references indicates that the range includes all the cells between the two cell references.
- **Formula:** An equation used in cells to perform mathematical calculations on its values.

Now that you are aware of some terms that refer to Excel, the next step is to become familiar with its interface. When you start Excel, your first step is to choose whether to start from a blank workbook, create it from pre-existing templates, or just edit a previously saved one. Carefully analyze Figure 5.7 to understand the main elements of the Excel interface.

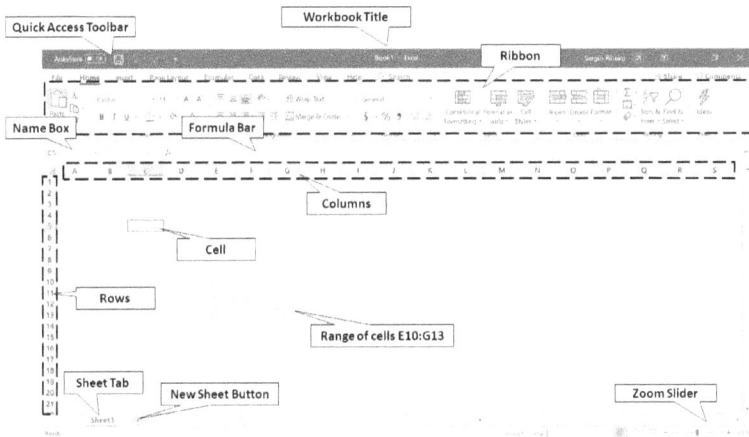

Figure 5.7 Excel interface

Some of the main components on your Excel interface are:

- **Quick Access Toolbar:** Lets you access common commands like AutoSave button to turn it on or off, Save, Undo, Redo, and Customized Quick Access Toolbar.
- **Workbook Title:** Shows the workbook filename.
- **Ribbon:** This is a user interface element located below the Quick Access Toolbar and the Title Bar. The Ribbon contains multiple tabs, each with several groups of commands like Home, Insert, Page Layout, Formulas, Data, Review, View, and Help.
- **Name Box:** Displays the name of the selected cell, table, chart, or object.
- **Formula Bar:** Displays the formula value or content in the active cell. It is also used to enter or edit the content.
- **Columns:** Lettered column headings.
- **Rows:** Numbered row headings.
- **Cell:** Column and row intersection used to insert data and formulas in your worksheet.

- **Sheet Tab:** Lets you know the selected or active worksheet.
- **New Sheet Button:** This button is used to create a new worksheet.
- **Zoom Slider:** It is used to zoom-in and zoom-out the worksheet.

Table 5.1 displays the important Excel shortcuts for operations.

Table 5.1 Excel shortcuts

Shortcut	Description
Ctrl + P	Used to open the print dialog window
Ctrl + N	Creates a new workbook
Ctrl + S	Saves the current workbook
Ctrl + C	Copy contents of current select
Ctrl + V	Paste data from the clipboard
Shift + F3	Displays the function insert dialog window
Shift + F11	Creates a new worksheet

Table 5.2 displays the important Excel shortcuts for navigation.

Table 5.2 Excel navigation shortcuts

Shortcut	Description
↑ ↓ → ←	Up, down, right, and left
Enter	Down one cell
Shift + Enter	Up one cell
PageUp	Up one fullscreen
PageDown	Down one fullscreen
Home	Move to column A from the current row
Ctrl + End	Move to the last cell in the column
Ctrl + Home	Move to cell A1
Tab	Right one cell
Shift + Tab	Left one cell

Let's create a worksheet to learn how to use the Excel interface and its features.

Part 1: Create a New Workbook and Insert Data

1. *Start Excel* and then click on the *Blank workbook* option.
2. In cell *A1*, type *Monthly Sales*.
3. Select the range *A3:A7* and type the following data pressing ENTER after each one:

   John
   Brenda
   Mary
   Richard
   Total

4. Select the range *B2:H2* and type the following data pressing ENTER after each one:

   Jan
   Feb
   Mar
   Apr
   May
   Jun
   Total

5. Select the range *B3:G6* and type the values as displayed in Figure 5.8, press ENTER after each one.

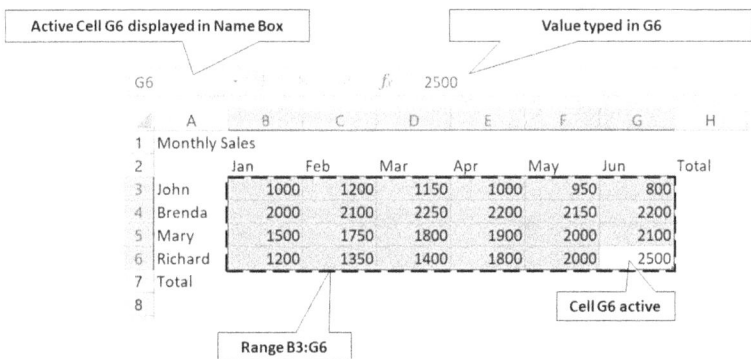

Figure 5.8 Inserting values in a select range of cells

6. Be sure the range *B3:G6* is still selected. Click *Quick Analysis* displayed in the right corner of the selected range. In the *Totals* tab, click on the first *Sum* button, and then click on the second *Sum* button. Compare your screen with Figure 5.9.

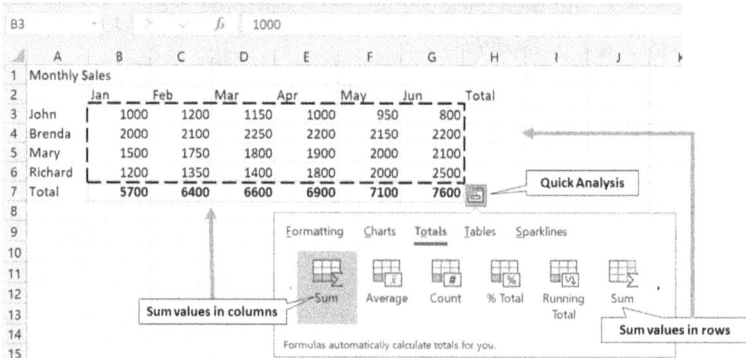

Figure 5.9 Inserting sum for the select range of cells

7. On the *Quick Access Toolbar*, click on the *Save* button and type *MyFirstWorkbook* as the filename for your document.

Part 2: Formatting

1. Select the range *A1:H1*, click on *Home tab*, in the *Font group*, click on *Bold*. In the *Alignment group*, click *Merge & Center*.
2. Select the range *B2:H2*, click on *Home tab*, in the *Font group*, click *Bold*. In the *Alignment group*, click *Align Right*.
3. Select the range *A3:H7*, click *Home tab*, in the *Font group*, in the *Borders* button select *All Borders*.
4. Select the range *A3:A7*, click on *Home tab*, in the *Font group*, click *Bold*.
5. Select the range *A7:H7*, click *Home tab*, in the *Font group*, in the *Fill Color* button select *Light Gray Background 2*.
6. Select the range *H2:H6*, click *Home tab*, in the *Font group*, in the *Fill Color* button, select *Light Gray Background 2*.
7. On the *Quick Access Toolbar*, click on the *Save* button.

Part 3: Creating charts

1. Select the range *B2:G3,* click *Insert tab*, in the *Charts group*, click on *Insert Line or Area Chart* and select *Line*. Drag and drop the chart on the best location in your worksheet. With the chart selected, click *Design tab*, then in the *Chart Styles group* select *Style 8*. Double click on *Chart Title* and change it to *JOHN'S SALES*.

2. Select the range *B2:G3,* click *Insert tab*, in the *Charts group*, click on *Insert Pie or Doughnut Chart* and select *Pie*. Drag and drop the chart on the best location in your worksheet. With the chart selected, click *Design tab*, then in the *Chart Styles group*, select *Style 8*. Double click on *Chart Title* and change it to *TOTAL SALES PER SELLER*.

3. Compare your screen with Figure 5.10.

4. On the *Quick Access Toolbar*, click on the *Save* button.

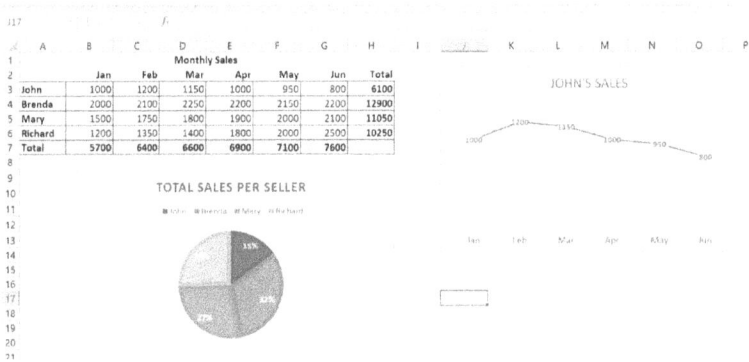

Figure 5.10 Creating charts

In the line chart displayed in Figure 5.10, you can see John's sales for the months from January to June. An analysis of the chart reveals that John's sales increased from January to February, but after decreased each month until June. This result could show a problem with John's sales.

In the pie chart displayed in Figure 5.10, you can see the total sales per seller. With 32 percent of the total sales, Brenda had the best performance compared to the other sellers. John, with only 15 percent, had the worst one.

Create a Presentation with Microsoft PowerPoint

Communication is a critical skill not only for your academic success, but also for your business career. When you have to communicate your ideas, presentation is everything, and Microsoft PowerPoint is one of the most efficient tools to help you. Microsoft PowerPoint, or only PowerPoint, is a widely used application for developing presentations. Through its means, you can create presentations simply and quickly. These presentations can use multimedia resources, such as sound, image, movement, animation, all combined so that you can achieve an interactive and effective presentation.

Among some of its main features, we can highlight the slide transition effects, the option of different types of letters, predefined presentation templates, audio and video resources, as well as the possibility of including animations.

Similar to Word and Excel, when you start PowerPoint, your first step is to choose whether to start from a blank presentation, create it from pre-existing templates, or just edit a previously saved one. Carefully analyze Figure 5.11 to understand the main elements of the PowerPoint interface.

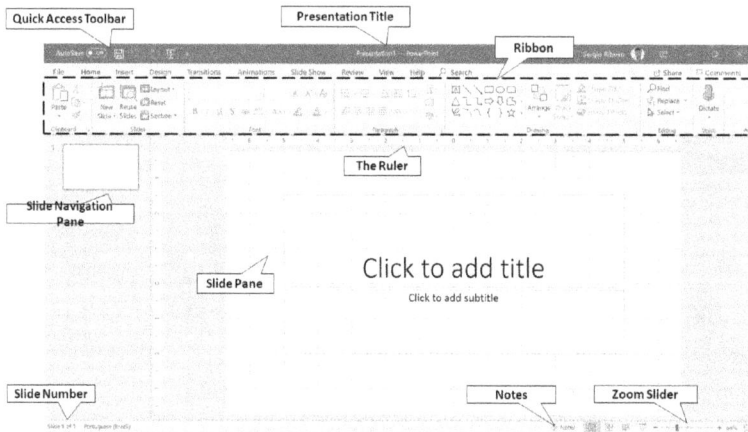

Figure 5.11 PowerPoint interface

Some of the main components on your PowerPoint interface are:

- **Quick Access Toolbar:** Lets you access common commands like the AutoSave button to turn it on or off, Save, Undo, Redo, and Customized Quick Access Toolbar.
- **Presentation Title:** Shows the presentation filename.
- **Ribbon:** This is a user interface element located below the Quick Access Toolbar and Title Bar. The Ribbon contains multiple tabs, each with several groups of commands like Home, Insert, Design, Transitions, Animations, Slide Show, Review, View, and Help.
- **Ruler:** Both rulers located at the top and to the left of your current slide make it easy to align text and objects on your slide.
- **Slide Pane:** This is your active slide where you can view and edit.
- **Slide Pane Navigation:** Allows you to display and organize the slides in your presentation. When you click on a slide, a thumbnail displays the slide in the Slide Pane.
- **Slide Number:** Displays your active slide as well as the total number of slides in your presentation.
- **Notes:** Displays an area bellow the Slide Pane where you can add notes to the active slide.
- **Zoom Slider:** It is used to zoom-in and zoom-out the Slide Pane.

Let create a presentation to learn how to use the PowerPoint interface and its features.

Part 1: Create a New Presentation and Insert Data

1. *Start PowerPoint* and click on *New*.
2. Click on the *Search box*, type *Facet* and press Enter.
3. Select the *Facet* theme. On the right of the *Facet preview*, you can see color variations associated with this theme.

4. Below *Facet preview*, click either *left* or *right-pointing* < *More images* > to see various types of slides look like in this theme.

5. After exploring the options of this theme, click on the *Create button* to start your new presentation.

6. In *Slide Pane*, click in the text *Click to add title* (this is the title placeholder) and type *Sales Report*.

7. Click in the subtitle placeholder and type *Monthly Sales from Jan to Jun.*

8. Click *Insert tab*, in the *Slides group*, click on *New Slide*.

9. In *Slide Pane* of the new slide, in the title placeholder, type *Total Sales per Month*.

10. In the content placeholder, click on the *Insert Table* icon and enter *7 columns* and *2 rows*. In the inserted table, enter the following data:

	Jan	Feb	Mar	Apr	May	Jun
Total	5,700	6,400	6,600	6,900	7,100	7,600

11. Select the table, click on the *Design tab*, in the *Table Styles group* select *Medium Style 3 – Accent 2*. Compare the result with Figure 5.12.

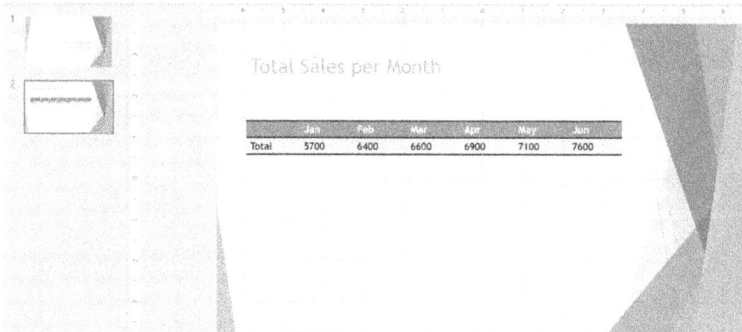

Figure 5.12 Total sales per month

12. Click *Insert tab*, in the *Slides group*, click on *New Slide*.

13. In *Slide Pane* of the new slide, in the title placeholder, type *Total Sales per Seller*.

14. In the content placeholder, click on *Insert Chart* and select *Pie* and click on the *OK button*.

15. Enter the data for the chart as displayed in Figure 5.13, when concluded close de spreadsheet window.

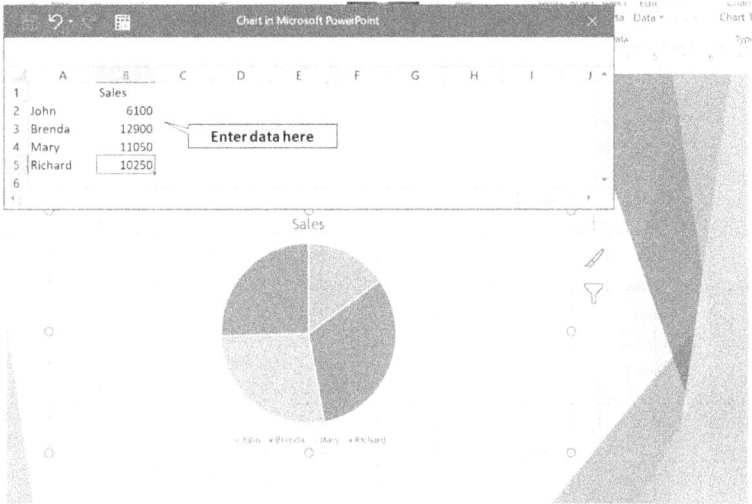

Figure 5.13 Entering data for the chart

16. Be sure the chart is selected, click on the *Design tab,* in the *Chart Styles group*, select *Style 8*.

17. Click on the *Slide Show tab*, in the *Start Slide Show group*, click on *From Beginning*. When running the slide show, press ENTER, SPACE BAR, ↓, or → on your keyboard to move to the next slide.

18. On the *Quick Access Toolbar,* click on the *Save* button, and type *MyFirstPresentation* as the filename for your document.

Part 2: Applying Transition and Animation

1. *Start PowerPoint* and click on *New*.

2. In the *Slide Pane Navigation,* select *Slide 1*, click on the *Transitions tab*, in the *Transitions to This Slide group*, select *Split*.

3. In the *Slide Pane Navigation,* choose *Slide 2*, click on the *Transitions tab*, in the *Transitions to This Slide group*, select *Peel Off*.

4. Select the *Title box*, click on the *Animations tab*, in the *Animation group*, select *Fly In*, in the *Timing group*, set *Star option* to *With Previous*, and *Duration* to *01.00*.

5. Select the *Table object*, click on the *Animations tab*, in the *Animation group*, select *Wipe*, in the *Timing group*, set *Star option* to *After Previous*, and *Duration* to *01.00.*

6. In the *Slide Pane Navigation*, choose *Slide 3*, click on the *Transitions tab*, in the *Transitions to This Slide group*, select *Switch*.

7. Select the *Title box*, click on the *Animations tab*, in the *Animation group*, select *Fly In*, in the *Timing group*, set *Star option* to *With Previous*, and *Duration* to *01.00.*

8. Select the *Chart object*, click on the *Animations tab*, in the *Animation group*, select *Swivel*, in the *Timing group*, set *Star option* to *After Previous*, and *Duration* to *02.00.*

9. Click on the *Slide Show tab*, in the *Start Slide Show group*, click on *From Beginning.*

10. On the *Quick Access Toolbar*, click on the *Save* button.

Summary

- Microsoft Office 2019 is a crucial software suite to help companies make more easy task management, and as a result, get things done more efficiently.
- Microsoft Word is a word processing program designed to help you create professional-quality documents.
- Excel is a spreadsheet editor that allows you to create tables, calculate and analyze data.
- PowerPoint is a widely used application for developing presentations.

Review Questions

1. When creating documents in Word, spreadsheets in Excel, or PowerPoint presentations, these files are temporarily stored in RAM. So, what should you do to transfer these files to your hard drive?

2. After giving a lecture on financial reports, John informed the employees present that he would make the slides for the talk available on the company's intranet so that everyone could have access. When he accessed the intranet and tried to upload the slide file created in Microsoft PowerPoint, he received the system message saying that the file format was invalid, and that he should convert or save the file to PDF format and try to perform the procedure again. How should John proceed to convert his slide file to PDF format?

Word Project: Flyer

Best4U Cafe will open a new coffee shop in Chicago at Bird Park residential area, at the corner of South Ave and Wood St. Create a flyer for the grand opening using a Word template.

1. *Start Word* and click on *New*.
2. Click on the *Search box* and type *grand opening flyer*.
3. Select the *Grand opening* template.
4. A new window will pop up, displaying information about the template. Click on *Create*.
5. When the document shows up, scroll down the screen to find the text—*FOURTH COFFEE*. Click on the text to replace it and type—*Best4U Cafe*.
6. Replace *At 9 AM* with At 5 PM.
7. Replace *November 10, 20XX* with *October 15, 2020*.
8. Replace *4567 Main St, Buffalo, NY 98052* with *9999 Main St, Chicago, IL*.
9. Replace *www.fourthcoffee.com* with *www.best4u.com*.
10. On the *Quick Access Toolbar*, click on the *Save* button, and type *Best4UCafeFlyer* as the filename for your document.
11. Click on the *File tab*, click on *Print* to display the *Print Preview*. Your completed document should look similar to Figure 5.14.

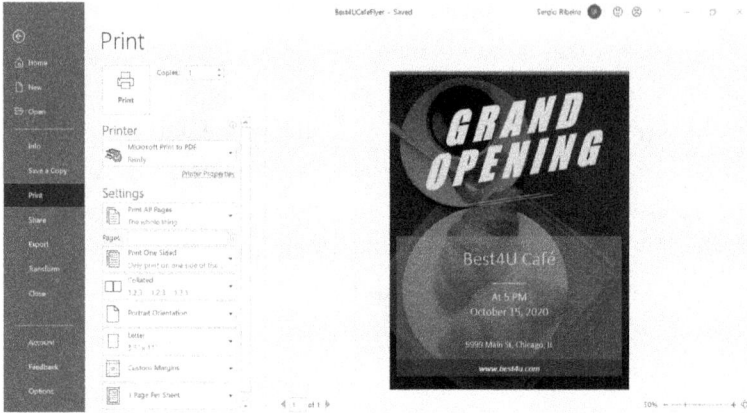

Figure 5.14 Best4UCafeFlyer document ended

Word Project: Resume

Resumes are used by employers to make hiring decisions. It is an essential tool for your job search where you can display your skills and qualities. In this project, you will create a resume using a Word template.

1. *Start Word* and click on *New*.
2. Click on the *Search box* and type *resume*.
3. Select the *Modern chronological resume* template.
4. Modify the resume typing over the text in the document to create your own. Change the generic data to include your personal and professional information.
5. Once you completed the editing, use Word tools for proofing.
6. Press CTRL + Home to move the insertion point to the top of your document.
7. Click on the *Review tab*, in *Proofing group*, click *Spelling & Grammar* to check spelling and grammar of your document.
8. On the *Quick Access Toolbar*, click *Save* and type *MyResume* as the filename.

Word Project: Cover Letter

When applying for an open position, a cover letter is a crucial way to tell an employer your qualifications for the post. It is an excellent opportunity to impress and get attention. In this project, you will create a cover letter using a Word template.

1. *Start Word* and click on *New*.
2. Click on the *Search box* and type *cover letter*.
3. Select the *Modern chronological cover letter* template.
4. Modify the cover letter typing over the text in the document to create your own. Change the generic data to include your personal and professional information.
5. Once you completed the edition, use Word tools for proofing.
6. Press CTRL + Home to move the insertion point to the top of your document.
7. Click on the *Review tab*, in *Proofing group*, click *Spelling & Grammar* to check spelling and grammar of your document.
8. On the *Quick Access Toolbar*, click *Save* and type *MyCoverLetter* as the filename.

Excel Project: Purchase Order

A purchase order or simply PO is an essential commercial document issued by a buyer to a seller indicating product, quantities, prices, and additional information related to purchase conditions and shipment. Also, it is used by the company to manage the purchasing of products and services from suppliers.

In this project, your challenge is to create the PO presented in Figure 5.15. Use learned knowledge and explore Excel to achieve new skills.

When you finish, *save* your workbook project as *MyPO*.

⊿	A	B	C	D	E	F
1	**PURCHASE ORDER**			Number: 709834		
2				Date: 15-Jun-20		
3						
4	Ordered by		Deliver to			
5						
6	Company Name		Customer Name			
7	999, Main St		888, North St			
8	City, State, ZIP		City, State, ZIP			
9	Country		Country			
10						
11	Phone:	999-090-0000	Phone:	999-090-0000		
12	Fax:	888-080-0000	Fax:	888-080-0000		
13	Contact:	Mr. Seller	Contact:	Mr. Customer		
14						
15	Part No.	Description	Quantity	Unit Price	Amount	Amount = Quantity * Unit Price
16	020-001	Notebook	2	680.00	1,360.00	
17	030-001	Printer	5	85.00	425.00	
18	025-010	Scanner	3	120.00	360.00	Total is the sum of amounts
19	Terms and conditions			Total	2,145.00	
20				Tax @ 7%	150.15	Tax is 7% of the Total
21				Shipping	35.00	
22				Grand Total	2,330.15	G. Total = Total + Tax + Shipping
23						

Figure 5.15 MyPO

Excel Project: Student Grade Book

A grade book is a handy tool used by teachers to record grades, calculate averages, and set student performance indicators.

In this project, you have to create the grade book presented in Figure 5.16. Your challenge is to discover how to use the function **IF()** to indicate when students pass or fail.

When you finish, *save* your workbook project as *MyGradeBook*.

	A	B	C	D	E	F	G	H	
1				**STUDENT GRADE BOOK**					
2									
3	#	ID	Name	Test 1	Test 2	Final Exam	Final Grade	Result	
4	1	30045	John	67	70	68	68	Pass	=IF()
5	2	30009	Richard	76	70	75	74	Pass	
6	3	30021	Mary	70	65	80	72	Pass	
7	4	30040	Brenda	45	30	50	42	Fail	
8	5	30022	Bell	80	78	82	80	Pass	
9								=AVG()	

Final Grade

Bell

Brenda

Mary

Richard

John

0 10 20 30 40 50 60 70 80 90

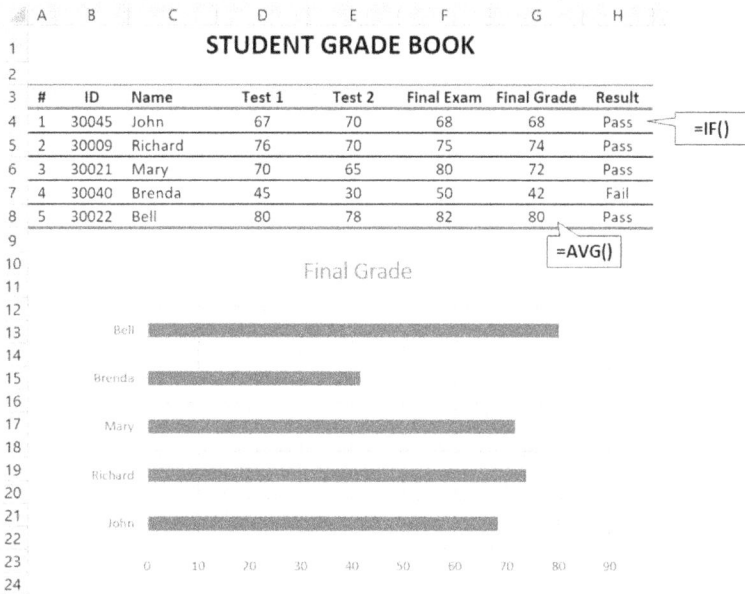

Figure 5.16 MyGradeBook

PowerPoint Project: Investment Presentation

You work in the accounts department, and your manager will make a presentation. In this project, you will create an investment presentation so that he can present it at the next meeting with possible investors.

1. *Start PowerPoint* and click on *New*.
2. Click on the *Search box*, type *Crop* and press Enter.
3. Select the *Crop Design* theme, then click on the *Create button* to start your new presentation.
4. In *Slide Pane Navigation*, select *Slide 1*.
5. In *Slide Pane*, click in the title placeholder, replace *Title Lorem Ipsum* with *Invest Consulting* and *Sit Dolor Amet* with *Mr. Johnson*.
6. In *Slide Pane Navigation*, select *Slide 2*, press DEL or Delete on your keyboard to remove the slide.
7. In the *Insert tab*, in the *Slides group*, click on *New Slide*.
8. Click in the title placeholder and type *Invest consulting*.
9. Click in the content placeholder and type:

- Own and independent management
- 15 years of investment experience
- Relationship-oriented services
- Quantitative investment process

10. In the *Insert tab*, in the *Slides group*, click on *New Slide*.
11. Click in the title placeholder and type *Invest consulting*.
12. In the content placeholder, click on the *SmartArt icon*, click on the *Process option*, and select *Continuous Block Process*. Be sure your *SmartArt* is selected, and click on the *Design tab*, in *Create Graphic group*, click on *Add Shape*. Edit your SmartArt to look like the following SmartArt (Figure 5.17).

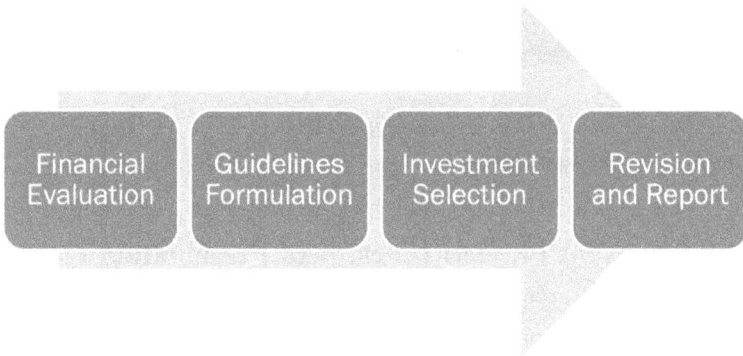

Figure 5.17 SmartArt for invest consulting slide

13. In the *Insert tab*, in the *Slides group*, click on *New Slide*.
14. Click in the title placeholder and type *Financial evaluation*.
15. In the content placeholder, click on the *SmartArt icon*, click on the *Process option*, and select *Chevron Accent Process*. Be sure the first shape of your *SmartArt* is selected, and press the key Delete remaining on two shapes. Edit your SmartArt to look like the following SmartArt (Figure 5.18).

Figure 5.18 SmartArt for financial evaluation slide

16. In the *Insert tab*, in the *Slides group*, click on *New Slide*.
17. Click in the title placeholder and type *Guidelines formulation*.
18. Be sure the content placeholder is selected. Click on the *Insert tab*, in the *Illustrations group*, click on *Icons*, click on the *Business option*, and select the following icon displayed (Figure 5.19).

Figure 5.19 Icon for guidelines formulation slide

19. Be sure your icon is selected. Click on the *Format tab*, in the *Size group*, change *Height* to *4"* and *Width* to *4"*. In the *Arrange group*, click on *Align* and select the *Align to Center option*.
20. In the *Insert tab*, in the *Slides group*, click on *New Slide*.
21. Click in the title placeholder and type *Investment selection*.
22. In the content placeholder, click on the *SmartArt icon*, click on the *Process option*, and select *Circle Process*. Edit your SmartArt to look like the following SmartArt (Figure 5.20).

Figure 5.20 SmartArt for investment selection slide

23. In the *Insert tab*, in the *Slides group*, click on *New Slide*.
24. Click in the title placeholder and type *Revision and report*.
25. In the content placeholder, click on the *SmartArt icon*, click on the *Cycle option*, and select *Cycle Arrow Process*. Be sure the first shape of your *SmartArt* is selected and press the key Delete remaining on two shapes. Edit your SmartArt to look like the following SmartArt (Figure 5.21).

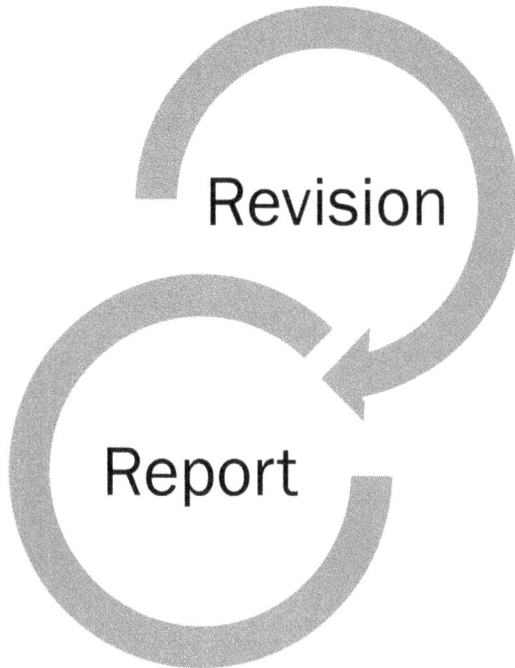

Figure 5.21 SmartArt for revision and report slide

26. In *Slide Pane Navigation*, select all *Slides*. Click on the *Transitions tab*, in the *Transitions to This Slide group*, select *Switch*.
27. On the *Quick Access Toolbar*, click on the *Save* button and type *InvestPresentation* as the filename for your document.

CHAPTER 6

Problem-Solving: Python

Learning Objectives
- Understand the Python programming environment
- Work with variables
- Use operators and expressions
- Understand the control structure
- Use IF
- Use FOR
- Use WHILE
- Create a function
- Create a class
- Implement and analyze data with Pandas

Python is a programming language created in the late 1980s. Its developer, Guido van Rossum, worked for Centrum Wiskunde and Informatica, located in the Netherlands, during the time of its introduction. Simple coding and a variety of resources have made this program a sought-after application in the language programming world. At the onset, this programming language was based on the ability to expand and has done so. Its developer, Guido van Rossum is now retiring with a version of Python 3.3 available to programmers.

There are some advantages to learning Python. This programming language has been on the top 10 list since 2003. It has 200,000 packages with a wide range of functionality. The most popular function is its platform portability. The majority of applications created are compatible with more than one operating system (OS).

The ability to interconnect with other programs on the market created before its inception makes it a top contender for the creation of new ideas. Upgrading existing applications with this program's emphasis on readability is a diversified product capable of implementation with ease. Add-ons have been accounted for as a win to programmers. With this feature of room for growth, Mr. van Russum's creation has been positioned to connect with programs not in production yet. This job security must not be overlooked for those willing to invest their time and skills into a career that has a future.

Figure 6.1 Woman programming on a notebook

Source: Christina Morillo/Pexels

Because of its simplicity and easy to learn code, this program has been noted as the most requested introductory course at top universities nationally. Well, sought-after programmers can expect an employment offer into an excellent salary for learning the ways of this specific programming. Noting partnerships with well-known websites such as Amazon, Facebook, and Instagram, the demand for those who can maintain these sites should not be refuted. Employment in gaming and software creation is not beyond the reach of one with skill and knowledge in a programming language. Add the understanding of a computer language in demand, and you have a winning hand.

With its influence on other programs, such as Boo, cobra, CoffeeScript, and others, understanding the logic of this language can influence a new skill set with other program languages as well.

Understand the Python Programming Environment

Python can be used for the development of desktop and Web solutions. It runs on different operating systems like Windows, Linux, Mac OS, Android, and so on. It is, therefore, an extremely flexible language.

Python programs can be run in Shell mode or through some integrated development environment (IDE). They can be developed using IDEs like Visual Studio, PyCharm, or Atom. But, they can also be written using a simple text editor, such as Windows Notepad.

Python is an interpreted, object-oriented, high-level programming language with dynamic semantics. So, for the execution of a Python program, there is a need for the interpreter. If you want to run a Python program on your computer, you must install Python on it. Installing Python on your computer will install not only the interpreter, but all the library packages needed for the most common functions.

There is also the possibility of using a Python environment without having to do any installation on your computer. In this case, the option would be to use a virtual environment where the entire Python environment is already configured and ready for use. Several Web platforms offer this option. For simplicity, we will use an online environment called Kaggle available at <www.kaggle.com>.

Kaggle is a free platform and an online community of data scientists and machine learning practitioners. To use the Kaggle online platform, it is necessary to create a Kaggle account (Figure 6.2).

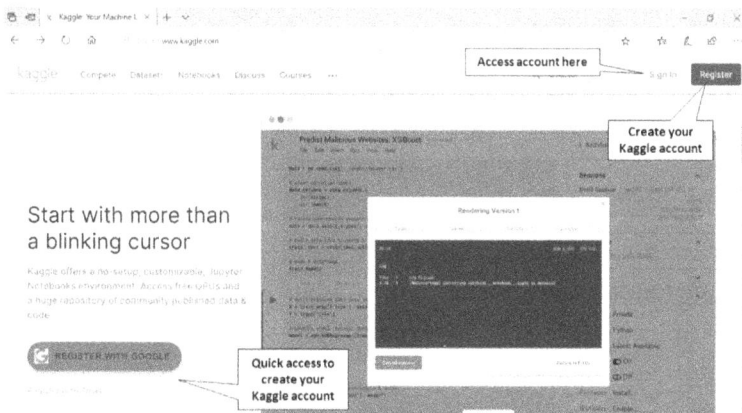

Figure 6.2 Kaggle website

How to Create a Kaggle Profile?

1. Go to the Kaggle website.
2. Click on the Register button.
3. Set up your Kaggle profile.

Also, you can create your Kaggle account with your Google account through the *Quick access* (Figure 6.2).

Once you have got your Kaggle account, you have to *Sign in* to your account to access your Kaggle environment (Figure 6.3).

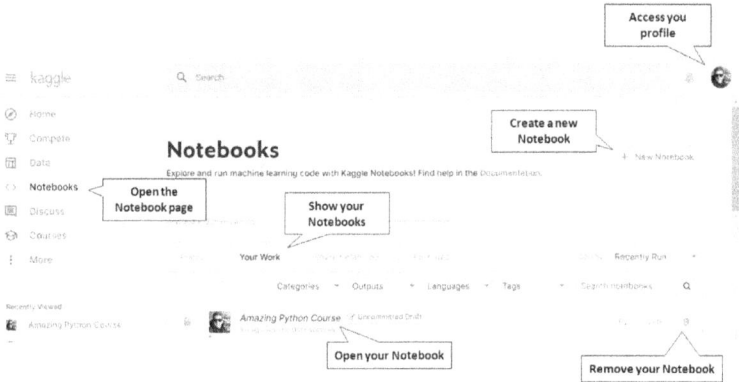

Figure 6.3 Your Kaggle environment

The purpose of using the Kaggle platform is this book is to learn how to create Python programs. You will need to create a Notebook to write and execute your Python programs. Once you have accessed your Kaggle account, click on the *Notebook option* on the left-side menu and compare Figure 6.3 with your browser and take the time to understand that.

How to Create a Notebook?

1. Access your Kaggle account.
2. On the left-side menu options, click on Notebook.
3. Click on +*New Notebook* (Figure 6.3).
4. On the new notebook page, set the options *Select language* to *Python* and *Select type* to *Notebook* (Figure 6.4).
5. Click on the *Create* button.

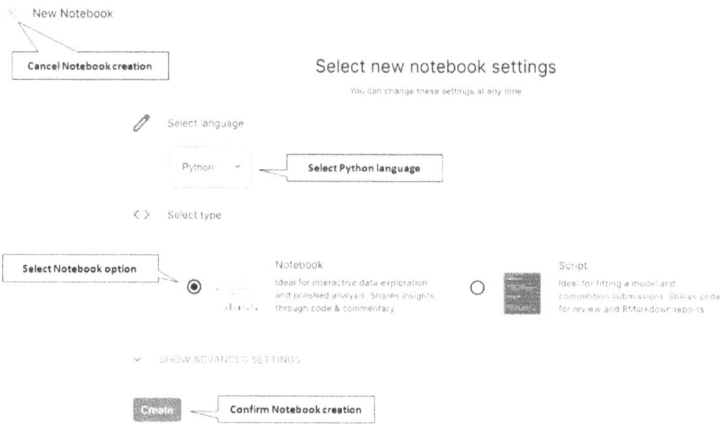

Figure 6.4 New notebook creation page

After you confirm the new notebook creation, you will get access to the notebook created. Look at Figure 6.5 and take the time to recognize those elements present on the new notebook creation page.

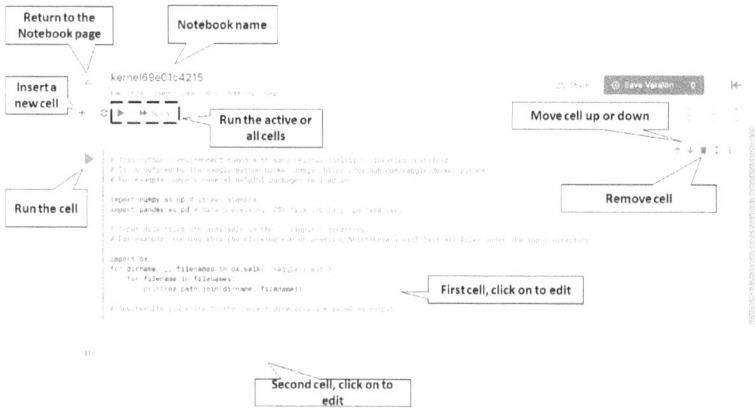

Figure 6.5 New notebook created

Note your new notebook will receive a standard name generated automatically (Figure 6.5); click on the notebook name and change it to *Python Course* or any other name of your preference. Also, the cell is the most critical part of your notebook area because it is there where you will write your Python code.

Now you are ready to develop your Python programs!

According to Webster, a computer program is a sequence of coded instructions that can be inserted into a mechanism, such as a computer
(Merriam-Webster.com Dictionary 2020).

A Python program put simply is a set of instructions telling the computer what to do in order to perform a particular task (Algorithm 6.1).

#	Algorithm 6.1

01
02
03
04
	`# This is a comment`
	
	`print("Hello, World!")`

	`Hello, World!`

Algorithm 6.1 displays a simple program with four lines of code and
two instruction lines. The instructions are also called statements.

Understanding Algorithm 6.1

- **Line 01:** The statement # *This is a comment* is a comment. In
  Python, a comment starts with the hash character (#). Comments are used to insert information on your code to make it
  more readable. Comments are ignored by Python interpreter.
- Line 03: The statement *print("Hello, World!")* is telling the
  computer to print the message *"Hello, World!"* in the output
  area.
- The last line with no number in the Algorithm 6.1 displays
  the output.

How to Create Your First Program on Kaggle?

1. Be sure you have your Python Course notebook opened.
2. Write the statements from Algorithm 6.1 to your Python Course
   notebook.
3. Click on icon Run cell to execute your program.

4. Compare your output results with Figure 6.6.

5. To show statement lines on your notebook click on the *View* in the options menu and select the *Toggle line numbers* option.

Figure 6.6 Python course notebook

Even though in this book we use the Kaggle platform as a development environment for your code and test, other environments can be used. In any different development environment, just type in the presented algorithm and execute it to check if the expected result is the same. Feel free to explore other Python development environments.

Work with Variables

In programming, a variable is an object or memory address capable of retaining and representing a value or expression. Variables only exist at run time and are associated with names (labels) called identifiers. A variable in Python can hold different data types, see Table 6.1.

Table 6.1 Python data types

Type	Description
int	Integers, a whole number such as 0, 1, 2, 15, and so on
float	Floating point, numbers with a decimal point
bool	Boolean, logical value indicating True or False
str	String, a sequence of characters
list	Lists, a sequence of objects
dict	Dictionaries, a sequence of objects Key: Value pairs
tup	Tuples, immutable sequence of objects
set	Sets, a collection of objects

In Algorithm 6.2 is presented a piece of code with some examples of variables.

#	Algorithm 6.2
01	# Working with variables
02	
03	studentName = "John"
04	credits = 120
05	grades = [85,70,75]
06	finalGrade = 76.67
07	approved = True
08	
09	print("The final grade obtained by", studentName, "was", finalGrade)
10	
	The final grade obtained by John was 76.67

Understanding Algorithm 6.2

- **Line 01:** Statement # Working with variables is a comment.
- **Line 03:** Statement *studentName* = *"John"* creates a string variable named *studentName* to hold the value *"John."*
- **Line 04:** Creation of an int variable called *credits* receiving the integer value *129*.
- **Line 05:** Creation of a list variable called *grades* receiving the list of three integer values *85, 70*, and *75*.
- **Line 06:** Creation of a float variable called *finalGrade* receiving the float value *76.67*.
- **Line 07:** Creation of a bool variable called *approved* receiving a logical Boolean value *True*.
- **Line 09:** Statement telling the computer to print a message with the student name and his final grade.
- The last line with no number in Algorithm 6.2 displays the output (execute this code into your Kaggle and compare the output).

To avoid an error when creating variable, it is crucial to be sure about Python variable naming rules:

- Must start with a letter or the underscore character
- Cannot begin with a number
- Can only contain alphanumeric characters and underscores (A-z, 0-9, and _)
- Variable names are case-sensitive

- Cannot be a Python keyword
- Should reflect its use
- When using more than one word for naming, use *camelCase* convention like *studentName* or *finalGrade*

The function *type()* can be used to know the variable data type. Also, in some cases, you need to convert the data type value of a variable to another one. The data type conversion can be done using the functions displayed in Table 6.2.

Table 6.2 List of functions for data type conversion

Function	Description
int(x)	Converts x to integer
float(x)	Converts x to float
str(x)	Converts x to string
list(x)	Converts x to list
tuple(x)	Converts x to tuple

In Algorithm 6.3 is presented a piece of code exemplifying how data type conversion works.

#	Algorithm 6.3
01	# Data type conversion
02	
03	tax = "2.5"
04	tax1 = float(tax)
05	
06	print(type(tax))
07	print(type(tax1))
08	
	`<class 'str'>` `<class 'float'>`

Understanding Algorithm 6.3

- **Line 03:** Statement *tax = "2.5"* creates a string variable named *tax* to hold the string value *"2.5."*
- **Line 04:** Creation of a float variable called *tax2* receiving the float value returned by the conversion of the variable tax by *float(tax)*.

- **Line 06:** Creation of a list variable called *grades* receiving the list of three integer values *85*, *70*, and *75*.
- **Line 06:** Print the data type for the variable *tax* using the function *type(tax)*.
- **Line 07:** Print the data type for the variable *tax1* using the function *type(tax1)*.

You can assign a value for a variable dynamically using the function *input()*, see Algorithm 6.4.

#	Algorithm 6.4
01	# Using the function input()
02	
03	studentName = input("Enter the Student Name:")
04	finalGrade = input("Enter the Student Final Grade:")
05	
	Enter the Student Name: John Enter the Student Final Grade: 76.50

In Algorithm 6.4, both created variables are string data types. In this case, the variable *finalGrade* could be converted to float using the function *float()*. There are two ways to do that, see Algorithms 6.5 and 6.6.

#	Algorithm 6.5
01	# Using the function input()
02	
03	finalGrade = input("Enter the Student Final Grade:")
04	finalGrade = float(finalGrade)
05	
	Enter the Student Final Grade: 76.50

#	Algorithm 6.6
01	# Using the function input()
02	
03	finalGrade = float(input("Enter the Student Final Grade:"))
04	
	Enter the Student Final Grade: 76.50

In the first example displayed in Algorithm 6.5, the conversion is made in two lines. In the second example presented in Algorithm 6.6, the conversion is made in one line. The second example is more compact. However, a little bit harder to read.

Use Operators and Expressions

When programming in Python, you will realize most of the statements written contain expressions. An expression is composed of operators and operands. In the given expression 5+7, the numbers 5 and 7 are called operands, and the symbol + is called the operator. So, the operators are the constructs used to manipulate the values of operands. Put it simply, operators are symbols that tell the Python interpreter to do some mathematical or logical operation.

Python operators are classified in groups, and most commons types of operators are displayed in Table 6.3.

Table 6.3 Python types of operators

Operator	Description	Example
Arithmetic		
+	Addition	x + y
-	Subtraction	x – y
*	Multiplication	x * y
/	Division	x / y
%	Modulus	x % y
**	Exponentiation	x ** y
//	Floor division	x // y
Assignment		
=	Assigns values from right-side operands to left-side operand	x = y assigns the value of y into x
+=	It adds right operand to the left operand and assigns the result to left operand	x += y is equivalent to x = x + y
-=	It subtracts right operand from the left operand and assigns the result to left operand	x -= y is equivalent to x = x – y
*=	It multiplies right operand with the left operand and assigns the result to left operand	x *= y is equivalent to x = x * y
/=	It divides left operand with the right operand and assigns the result to left operand	x /= y is equivalent to x = x / y
%=	It takes modulus using two operands and assigns the result to left operand	x %= y is equivalent to x = x % y
**=	Performs exponential (power) calculation on operators and assign value to the left operand	x **= y is equivalent to x = x ** y
//=	It performs floor division on operators and assigns value to the left operand	x //= y is equivalent to x = x // y

Table 6.3 Python types of operators

Comparison		
==	Equal, if the values of two operands are equal, then the condition becomes true	(x == y)
!=	Not equal, if the values of two operands are not equal, then the condition becomes true	(x != y)
<>	Not equal, If the values of two operands are not equal, then the condition becomes true.	(x <> y)
>	Greater than, if the value of the left operand is greater than the value of the right operand, then the condition becomes true	(x > y)
<	Less than, if the value of the left operand is less than the value of the right operand, then the condition becomes true	(x < y)
>=	Greater than or equal to, if the value of the left operand is greater than or equal to the value of the right operand, then the condition becomes true	(x >= y)
<=	Less than or equal to, if the value of the left operand is less than or equal to the value of right operand, then condition becomes true	(a <= b)
Logical		
and	Returns true if both the operands are true	(x and y)
or	Returns true if one of the operands is true	(a or b)
not	Reverse the result, returns false if the result is true	not (a and b)
Identity		
is	Returns true if both operands are the same object	x is y
is not	Returns true if both operands are not the same object	x is not y
Membership		
in	Returns true if it finds an operand inside the other one	x in y
not in	Returns true if it does not find an operand inside the other one	x not in y

The order of operations follows the mathematics, which means the multiplication is evaluated before the addition. So, the expression 2+3*2 results in 8, not 10. Similar to the mathematics, you can use parentheses to override the usual order. In this case, (2+3)*2 results in 10, not 8.

#	Algorithm 6.7

```
01  x = 10                    # assigning value 10 to x
02  y = 15                    # y is receiving 15
03  z = [5,10,25]
04  x += y
05
06  print(x)
07  print(y)
08  print(x > y)              # comparison
09  print(x==y and x>y)       # logical
10  print(x==y or x>y)        # logical
11  print(x is y)             # identity
12  print(x is not y)         # identity
13  print(x in z)             # membership
14
```

```
25
15
True
False
True
False
True
True
```

Algorithm 6.7 gives some examples of how to use the operators. Test the code on your Python environment, analyze, and compare the results.

Understand the Control Structure

A program as a set of instructions represents a particular implementation of an algorithm. The goal of building an algorithm is to define a problem-solving strategy. The steps outlined in the algorithm to solve the problem are structured in the form of commands and statements that indicate the intended use of variables. This problem-solving strategy in the form of an algorithm is structured in blocks of code. And, its execution occurs in an orderly manner following the predefined steps. In this way, we can say that this execution follows a flow structure where each statement to be executed is preceded by another.

A control structure (or flow of control) refers to the order in which instructions, expressions, and function calls are executed or evaluated. The types of flow control structure available can be classified as a sequence, selection, and iteration.

Sequence, also called sequential flow, is the natural flow where the commands are executed sequentially, following the order in which they were declared in the source code (Figure 6.7).

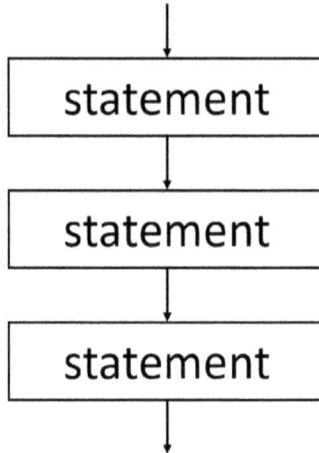

Figure 6.7 Sequence control structure

#	Algorithm 6.8
01	orderNumber = 9025
02	itemId = 1045
03	itemDescription = "Motherboard"
04	itemPrice = 125.50
05	itemQuantity = 5
06	total = itemPrice * itemQuantity
07	
08	print("Order Number:",orderNumber)
09	print("Item ID:",itemId)
10	print("Description:",itemDescription)
11	print("Price:",itemPrice)
12	print("Quantity:",itemQuantity)
13	print("Total:",total)
14	
	Order Number: 9025
	Item ID: 1045
	Description: Motherboard
	Price: 125.5
	Quantity: 5
	Total: 627.5

Sequential execution of statements, one line after another like following a recipe, is the default mode. In Algorithm 6.8, all statements will be executed starting at line 01 and ending at line 13, one line after another.

Selection, also called conditional flow, is a structure where different actions will be performed depending on whether the selection (or condition) is true or false. In this structure, a conditional command defines a fork in the flow. The condition is an expression that will be processed and transformed into a Boolean value, that is, true or false. Thus, once the alternative is executed, then the execution flow is resumed in the command that succeeds that conditional command (Figure 6.8).

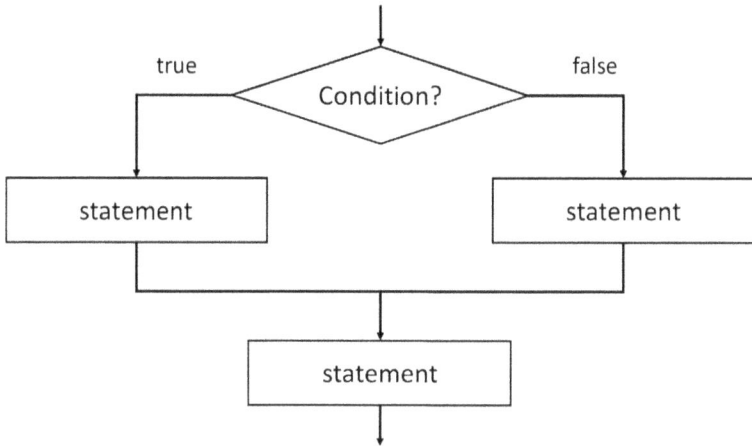

Figure 6.8 Selection control structure

In Python, the conditional structure is implemented through the IF command with single, double, or multiple alternatives.

Iteration, also called repetition or repetitive flow, this structure allows you to execute the same block of statements more than once, according to a condition or a counter. In this structure, a repetitive command implements cyclic executions of a block of codes. When the condition is no longer met, the cycle is interrupted, and the execution flow is then resumed in the statement that succeeds the repetitive structure (Figure 6.9).

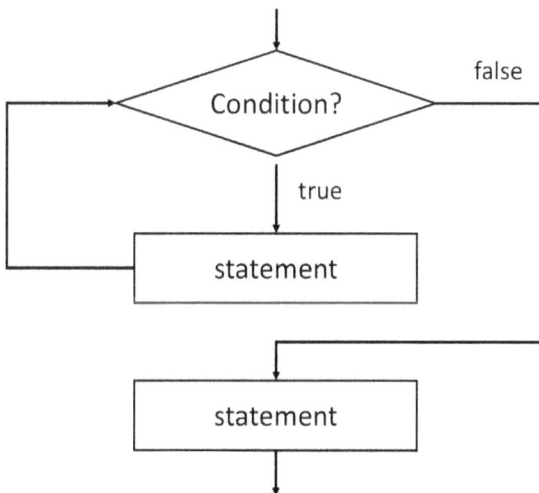

Figure 6.9 Iteration control structure

In Python, a repetitive flow structure is implemented through the repeat-FOR or repeat-WHILE structure.

Use IF

The *IF* statement is an example of a conditional structure used when we need to decide whether a code block should be executed or not. It is associated with a condition and the code block that will be executed if the condition value is true. This command can be implemented with single, double, or multiple alternatives.

Single Alternative Syntax

```
if <condition>:
        <indented statements>
```

#	Algorithm 6.9
01	# Single alternative
02	
03	age = int(input("How old are you (use numbers)? "))
04	
05	if (age < 18):
06	print("Sorry, you cannot drive!")
07	
	How old are you (use numbers)? 15 Sorry, you cannot drive!

Test Algorithm 6.9 and enter 15 for the question. Because the variable age will receive the value 15, the condition *(age < 18)* will return true, and the statement inside the IF structure will be executed. Otherwise, entering an age equal to or greater than 18, the condition will return false.

Double Alternatives Syntax

if <condition>:

>   <indented statements>

>   else:

>   >   <indented statements>

#	Algorithm 6.10

01
02
03
04
05
06
07
08
09
	`# Double alternatives`
	
	`score = int(input("Enter your score: "))`
	
	`if (score > 49):`
	`        print("Pass")`
	`else:`
	`        print("Fail")`

	`Enter your score: 75` `Pass`

Test Algorithm 6.10 and enter *75* for the score. Because the variable *score* will receive the value *75*, the condition *(score > 49)* will return true, and the statement inside the IF structure will be executed. Otherwise, entering a score equal to or less than 49, the condition will return false, and the message "Fail" will be printed.

Multiple Alternatives Syntax

if <condition>:

>   <indented statements>

>   elif <condition>:

>   >   <indented statements>

>   elif <condition>:

>   >   <indented statements>

#	Algorithm 6.11
01	# Multiple alternatives
02	
03	n1 = int(input("Enter the first #: "))
04	n2 = int(input("Enter the second #: "))
05	
06	if (n1 > n2):
07	print("First # is greater than second #")
08	elif (n1 == n2):
09	print("First # is equal to second #")
10	else:
11	print("First # is less than second #")
12	
	Enter the first #: 25 Enter the second #: 25 First # is equal to second #

Test Algorithm 6.11 and enter *25* for the first and second numbers and analyze the result. Try entering different values and verify the results.

Consider This Problem

You have to create a program to sum two given integers. However, if the sum is between 10 and 15, it will return 15. How does this program look like?

You can find the solution to this problem in Algorithm 6.12.

#	Algorithm 6.12
01	n1 = int(input("Enter the first integer: "))
02	n2 = int(input("Enter the second integer: "))
03	sum = n1+n2
04	
05	if sum in range(10,15):
06	print(15)
07	else:
08	print(sum)
09	
	Enter the first integer: 7 Enter the second integer: 8 15 Enter the first integer: 3 Enter the second integer: 2 5

Execute Algorithm 6.12 for testing. In the first execution, enter the integers 7 and 8, the result should be 15. In the second execution, enter the integers 3 and 2, the result should be 5.

Use FOR

The *FOR* statement is the most used repetition structure in Python. It can be used with a numeric sequence generated with the range() function or associated with a list. The repetition code snippet is executed for each value of the number sequence or the list. In other programming languages, this command has the purpose of performing an iteration based on an arithmetic progression, going through the numbers defined by the user. In Python, the iteration is done going through the items of a sequence. This sequence can be from a list or even a string.

Syntax

for <variable> in range(start, stop, step):

    <indented statements>

Or

for <variable> in list:

    <indented statements>

#	Algorithm 6.13
| 01<br>02<br>03<br>04<br>05 | ```python
tickets = int(input("How many tickets do you want to print? "))

for ticket in range(0,tickets):
      print("Ticket #", ticket)
``` |
|  | ```
How many tickets do you want to print? 5
Ticket # 0
Ticket # 1
Ticket # 2
Ticket # 3
Ticket # 4
``` |

Test Algorithm 6.13 and enter 5 for the numbers of tickets and analyze the result. Note the first ticket number starts from 0. Do you know how to start from 1 instead?

Consider This Problem

Based on the salaries displayed in Table 6.4, create a payroll report to list the names, wages, and total payroll at the end of the report.

Table 6.4 List of employee and wages

Employee	Salary
John	45000
Mary	30000
Luke	55000

You can find the solution to this problem in Algorithm 6.14.

#	Algorithm 6.14
01	`payroll = [["John",45000],["Mary",30000],["Luke",55000]]`
02	`total = 0`
03	
04	`for employee, salary in payroll:`
05	`    print(employee, salary)`
06	`    total += salary`
07	
08	`print("Total:",total)`
09	

	`John 45000`
	`Mary 30000`
	`Luke 55000`
	`Total: 130000`

Execute Algorithm 6.14 for testing and analysis.

Use WHILE

The *WHILE* statement is another type of repetition structure. This statement has the function to repeat a block of code as long as a given part is satisfied. Therefore, the loop or repetition is directly associated with a condition. In other words, as long as the condition has a true value, the block of code is executed. When the condition has a false value, the repetition ends.

Syntax

while <condition>:

    <indented statements>

#	Algorithm 6.15
01	`stay = True`
02	
03	`while stay:`
04	`    print("---------------------------------------")`
05	`    print("<A>dd <R>emove <L>ist <E>xit")`
06	`    option = input()`
07	`    if option in "Aa":`
08	`        print("Adding...")`
09	`    elif option in "Rr":`
10	`        print("Removing...")`
11	`    elif option in "Ll":`
12	`        print("Listing...")`
13	`    elif option in "Ee":`
14	`        stay = False`
15	`    else:`
16	`        print("Invalid option")`
17	
18	`print("Program ended")`
19	

```
---------------------------------------
<A>dd <R>emove <L>ist <E>xit
a
Adding...
---------------------------------------
<A>dd <R>emove <L>ist <E>xit
r
Removing...
---------------------------------------
<A>dd <R>emove <L>ist <E>xit
l
Listing...
---------------------------------------
<A>dd <R>emove <L>ist <E>xit
x
Invalid option
---------------------------------------
<A>dd <R>emove <L>ist <E>xit
e
Program ended
```

Test Algorithm 6.15. Enter the letters *a*, *r*, *l*, *x*, and *e* and check how the program works. Note at line 07 was used the condition *(option in "Aa")* instead of *(option == "A")*. The condition *(option in "Aa")* works better because the user does not need to care about typing the option in the lower or upper case. The condition *(option == "A")* will return false when the user types *a* (lower case) rather than *A* (upper case). The reason is that Python is case sensitive, so *a* and *A* are different.

Consider This Problem

Create a program to read a password until it is correct. When a wrong password is entered, print *Access denied. Try again!* If the right password is entered, print *Access granted!* Then, quit the loop. The correct password is 43210.

You can find the solution to this problem in Algorithm 6.16.

#	Algorithm 6.16

01
02
03
04
05
06
07
08
09
10
	`savedPwd = "43210"`
	`typedPwd = " "`
	
	`while (typedPwd != savedPwd):`
	`    typedPwd = input("Password: ")`
	`    if typedPwd == savedPwd:`
	`        print("Access granted!")`
	`    else:`
	`        print("Access denied. Try again!")`

	`Password: 1234`
	`Access denied. Try again!`
	`Password: 43210`
	`Access granted!`

Test Algorithm 6.16, enter 1234 for the password int the first time and check the message. Note the program will still running until you enter the correct password, then enter 43210 for the password to get access granted and end the program.

Create a Function

One of the main purposes of a programming language is to automate actions making them faster. When a certain action that is large is used frequently, we have the option of creating a function that fulfills its objective. This way, you can reduce the space occupied by our final program, in addition to leaving it with a cleaner appearance, as the code size will decrease. These functions also help in the task of debugging your code, as you will not need to search the code for the error, just enter the function, and modify it. Put it simply, a function is a block of organized and reusable code used to perform a specific action, only running when it is called. Functions receive data through its parameters and return data as a result.

Syntax

def function_name(<parameters>):

    <indented statements>

    return <result>

#	Algorithm 6.17
01	# 1) Defining the functions
02	
03	# Function without parameters and return
04	def greeting():
05	print("Hello from my function")
06	
07	# Function with parameters and return
08	def sum(a, b, c):
09	total = a+b+c
10	return total
11	
12	# 2) Calling the functions
13	x = sum(5,10,2)
14	y = sum(7,7,6)
15	
16	greeting()
17	print(x)
18	print(y)
19	greeting()
20	
	Hello from my function
	17
	20
	Hello from my function

Algorithm 6.17 gives an example of how to define and use functions. In this example were created two functions, *greeting()* and *sum()*. At lines 16 and 19, the function greeting() is called. At lines 17 and 18, the function sum() is called with different values for its parameters. Test and study the algorithm.

Consider This Problem

Create a function to calculate and return the total payroll for the list presented in Table 6.4. The payroll list has to be passed as a parameter to the function.

#	Algorithm 6.18
01	# Defining the Function
02	def payroll_sum(pList):
03	total = 0
04	for employee, salary in pList:
05	total+=salary
06	return total
07	
08	payroll = [["John",45000],["Mary",30000],["Luke",55000]]
09	
10	print("Total:",payroll_sum(payroll))
11	
	Total: 130000

Execute Algorithm 6.18 for testing and analysis.

Create a Class

The concept of class and objects are related to some families of programming languages. They are structured languages within the idea of object-oriented programming. Within this concept, a class is a structure that abstracts a set of objects with similar characteristics. A class defines the object's behavior through its methods, and object's states through its attributes. Simply put, a class describes the actions of its objects and what information they can store. A class is an object design. An object is an instance of a class.

Syntax

```
class ClassName:
   <indented statements>

   def metodName(self, <parameters> )
      <indented statements>
      return <result>
```

#	Algorithm 6.19

```
01  # Defining the class
02  class Student:
03      name = ""
04      phone = ""
05      email = ""
06      grades = []
07
08      def getFinalGrade(self):
09          final = 0
10          for grade in self.grades:
11              final+=grade
12          final = final/len(self.grades)
13          return final
14
15
16  # Instantiating a class/creating objects
17
18  s1 = Student()
19  s1.name = "Peter"
20  s1.phone = "999-9999"
21  s1.email = "peter@email.com"
22  s1.grades = [75,85,80]
23
24  s2 = Student()
25  s2.name = "Anna"
26  s2.phone = "999-9988"
27  s2.email = "anna@email.com"
28  s2.grades = [86,78,82]
29
30
31  print(s1.name, " > ", s1.getFinalGrade() )
32  print(s2.name, " > ", s2.getFinalGrade() )
33
```

```
Peter  >  80.0
Anna   >  82.0
```

Algorithm 6.19 displays how to create a class and instantiate the class to create an object. A class named Student is defined starting at line 02 and ending at line 13. The class has four attributes called name, phone, e-mail, and grades. In the class, a method was defined as getFinalGrade() that calculated the average of the grades returning the result. Two Student objects were created in lines 18 and 24.

Consider This Problem

Create a class to implement a bank account. The class must have the following attributes: account number, account type, balance, and transaction history. The methods are as follows: deposit, withdraw, and statement. The deposit and withdraw methods must update the balance and transaction history with each transaction.

#	Algorithm 6.20

```
01  # Defining the class
02  class BankAccount:
03      accNumber = ""
04      accType = "Chequing"
05      accBalance = 0
06      accStatement = []
07
08      def deposit(self,date,amount):
09          self.accStatement.append(["[+]",date,amount])
10          self.accBalance += amount
11
12      def withdraw(self,date,amount):
13          self.accStatement.append(["[-]",date,amount])
14          self.accBalance -= amount
15
16      def statement(self):
17          print(self.accType,"Account #",self.accNumber)
18          for op,date,amount in self.accStatement:
19              print(op,date,amount)
20          print("[=] Balance >>",self.accBalance)
21
22
23  # Instantiating the class/creating objects
24  cheq = BankAccount()
25  cheq.accNumber = "99999-0"
26  cheq.deposit("05-15-2020",150)
27  cheq.deposit("05-17-2020",170)
28  cheq.withdraw("05-18-2020",50)
29  cheq.deposit("05-19-2020",180)
30  cheq.withdraw("05-25-2020",200)
31  cheq.statement()
32
```

```
Chequing Account # 99999-0
[+] 05-15-2020 150
[+] 05-17-2020 170
[-] 05-18-2020 50
[+] 05-19-2020 180
[-] 05-25-2020 200
[=] Balance >> 250
```

Note the attribute for account transaction historical is a list data type called accStatement. This attribute stores the operation, date, and amount for each deposit or withdraw. By default, the accType is a chequing account. The method statement() prints the account statement with all account information.

Implement and Analyze Data with Pandas

Because of its maturity and a huge community, Python already has a set of functions ready to be used. Thinking about reusing code, without the need to reinvent the wheel, we have at your disposal a vast collection of Python libraries. These libraries are grouped into structures called modules. These modules can be easily imported and incorporated into your program.

Syntax

import <module> as <alias>

One of these available modules is the Pandas library (Figure 6.10). This Python library provides structures and data analysis tools. With a simple interface and powerful resources, this library has become one of the most used for data analysis.

Figure 6.10 Pandas logo

Source: PyData Development Team

Pandas is a high-level data manipulation tool built on the Numpy package, and its main data structures are called Series and DataFrame.

Series

Pandas Series is like a one-dimensional labeled array, a list of values, capable of holding any data type. Every series has an axis label, the index, which gives tags to each element of the list.

#	Algorithm 6.21
01	`import pandas as pd`
02	
03	`sales = pd.Series([5700,6400,6600,6900,7100,7600],`
04	`                  index=["Jan","Feb","Mar","Apr","May","Jun"])`
05	
06	`print(sales)`
07	
08	`print("Total",sales.sum())`
09	`print("Average",sales.mean())`
10	
11	`sales.plot.line()`
12	

```
Jan      5700
Feb      6400
Mar      6600
Apr      6900
May      7100
Jun      7600
dtype: int64
Total 40300
Average 6716.666666666667
```

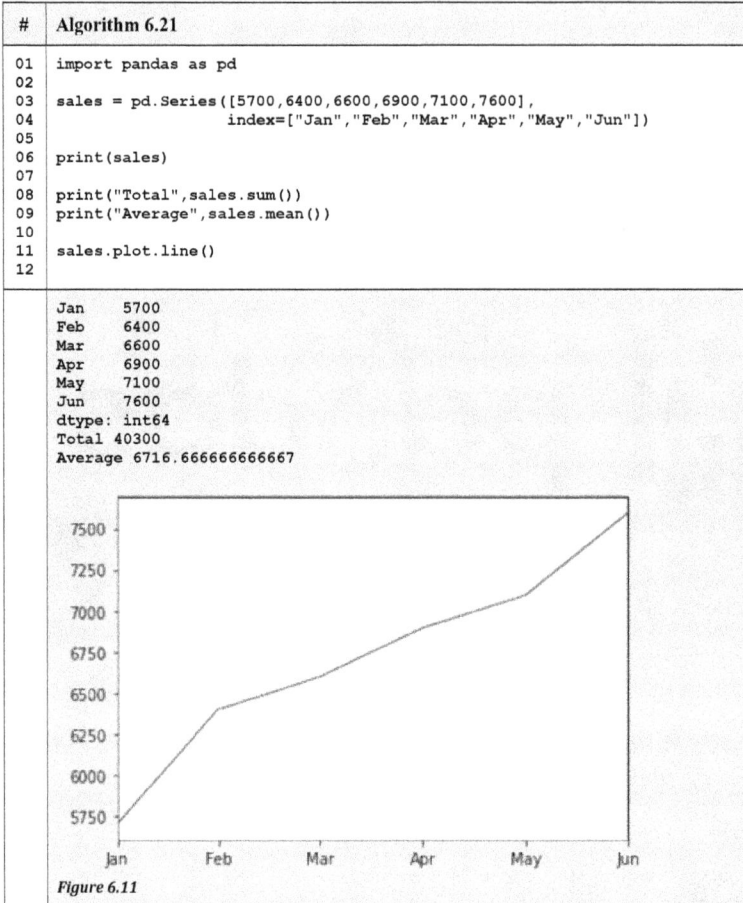

Figure 6.11

Execute Algorithm 6.21 for testing and analysis. At line 01, the Pandas module is imported and called *pd*. A Series data type is created at line 03, named as sales with two columns displayed by the print() function at line 06. At lines 08 and 09, the sum and average of the values are displayed. At line 08, a line chart is plotted. You can use the methods pie() and bar() to display a pie or bar chart.

DataFrame

Pandas DataFrame is a two-dimensional structure of data, like a spreadsheet, composed of rows and columns, with several functionalities for processing and analyzing data, such as aggregation and counts. This data type allows you to store and manipulate tabular data in rows of observations and columns of variables.

#	Algorithm 6.22
01	`import pandas as pd`
02	
03	`payroll = pd.DataFrame([["John",45000],["Mary",30000],["Luke",55000]])`
04	`payroll.columns = ["Employee","Salary"]`
05	
06	`print(payroll)`
07	
	``` Employee Salary 0 John 45000 1 Mary 30000 2 Luke 55000```

Algorithm 6.22 shows how to implement code using Pandas DataFrame. In a few lines, it is possible to get a DataFrame. At line 03, a DataFrame called payroll was created. At line 04, the columns were labeled, column 1 as Employee and column 2 for Salary. The payroll DataFrame is displayed in the output area if you include in your program the method *payroll.describe()* you can get an overview of your data. Also, you can rank the salary column using the method rank() adding *payroll["Salary"].rank()* to your program.

Consider This Problem

Create a program to implement the DataFrame presented in Figure 6.12. Based on the information of the DataFrame, answer the following questions:

1. How many units are available for sale and rent?
2. What is the cheapest rental property?
3. What is the most expensive property for sale?
4. List the properties available in NY.

	deal	type	bedroom	bathroom	built	location	price
0	rent	apt	2	1	2000	NY	1500
1	sale	apt	3	1	1950	FL	300000
2	sale	condo	2	1	1970	FL	250000
3	sale	home	4	2	1980	FL	280000
4	rent	condo	2	1	2005	NY	1600
5	rent	apt	1	1	2010	CA	1350
6	rent	apt	2	1	1990	CA	1700
7	sale	home	3	1	1985	NY	245000
8	rent	home	2	1	2010	NY	1200
9	sale	home	2	1	1960	CA	380000

Figure 6.12 Properties dataframe

#	Algorithm 6.23

```
01  import pandas as pd
02
03  data = { "deal" : ["rent","sale","sale","sale","rent","rent",
04                     "rent","sale","rent","sale"],
05           "type" : ["apt","apt","condo","home","condo","apt","apt",
06                     "home","home","home"],
07           "bedroom" : [2,3,2,4,2,1,2,3,2,2],
08           "bathroom" : [1,1,1,2,1,1,1,1,1,1],
09           "built" : [2000,1950,1970,1980,2005,2010,1990,1985,2010,1960],
10           "location" : ["NY","FL","FL","FL","NY","CA","CA",
11                         "NY","NY","CA"],
12           "price" : [1500,300000,250000,280000,1600,1350,1700,
13                      245000,1200,380000]}
14
15  properties = pd.DataFrame(data)
16
17  prop_group = properties.groupby("deal") #group the properties by deal
18
19  q1 = prop_group["type"].count()
20  q2 = prop_group.get_group("rent")
21       [properties.price==properties["price"].min()]
22  q3 = prop_group.get_group("sale")
23       [properties.price==properties["price"].max()]
24  q4 = properties[properties.location=="NY"]
25
26  print("1. How many units are available for sale and rent?")
27  print(q1)
28
29  print("\n2. What is the cheapest rental property?")
30  print(q2)
31
32  print("\n3. What is the most expensive property for sale?")
33  print(q3)
34
35  print("\n4. List the properties available in NY")
36  print(q4)
37
```

```
1. How many units are available for sale and rent?
deal
rent    5
sale    5
Name: type, dtype: int64

2. What is the cheapest rental property?
   deal  type  bedroom  bathroom  built  location  price
8  rent  home        2         1   2010        NY   1200

3. What is the most expensive property for sale?
   deal  type  bedroom  bathroom  built  location   price
9  sale  home        2         1   1960        CA  380000

4. List the properties available in NY
```

Understanding Algorithm 6.23

- **Line 03:** Statement in this line creates a dict variable named *data* to be used by Pandas DataFrame method at line 15.
- **Line 17:** Creation of a grouped Pandas DataFrame called *prop_group*.
- **Line 19:** Units are counted per type and result is stored in the variable *q1*.
- **Line 20:** A filter to get the minimal price for the group rent is applied and result stored in the variable *q2*.
- **Line 22:** A filter to get the maximum price for the group sale is applied and result stored in the variable *q3*.
- **Line 23:** A filter to get properties where the location equals to "NY" is applied and result stored in the variable *q4*.

Execute Algorithm 6.23 for testing and analysis.

Summary

- Python is a programming language created in the late 1980s by Guido van Rossum and can be used for the development of desktop and Web solutions.
- Kaggle is a free platform and an online community of data scientists and machine learning practitioners.
- A variable is an object or memory address capable of retaining and representing a value or expression.
- Operators are symbols that tell the Python interpreter to do some mathematical or logical operation.
- A control structure (or flow of control) refers to the order in which instructions, expressions, and function calls are executed or evaluated.
- A function is a block of organized and reusable code used to perform a specific action, only running when it is called.
- A class describes the actions of its objects and what information they can store.
- Pandas is a library that provides structures and data analysis tools.

Review Questions

1. What are the rules essential to remember when naming variables?
2. What is the output of the following code:

$$x = 10$$
$$y = 2$$
$$x \mathrel{+}= y^*(x+5)$$

3. Describe the following code:

$$x = \text{Schedule}()$$

4. What kind of business problem can be solved with Python?
5. Why should a business professional learn Python?

Python Project: Finding an Employee in a Given List

Create a function to find an employee in the list presented in Table 6.4 and return the employee's salary. Name the function as *getSalary()*. For example, the command *getSalary(payroll, "John")* will return *45000*. If the name is not found, the function will return *None*.

Solution

#	Algorithm 6.24
01	# Defining the Function
02	def getSalary(pList,pName):
03	rSalary = None
04	for employee, salary in pList:
05	if employee == pName:
06	rSalary = salary
07	return rSalary
08	
09	payroll = [["John",45000],["Mary",30000],["Luke",55000]]
10	employee = "John"
11	salary = getSalary(payroll,employee)
12	
13	if salary == None:
14	print(employee, "salary was not found in the list")
15	else:
16	print("The salary of ",employee," is ",salary)
17	
	The salary of John is 45000

Execute Algorithm 6.24, passing different names for testing and analysis.

Python Project: Payroll Data Management

Create a program to manage payroll data following the rules:

1. The program starts with an options menu where the user should type the letter "A" for adding a new employee in the payroll list, "R" to remove an employee from the payroll, "L" to print the payroll list, and "E" to exit the program.
2. The main functionalities of the program should be inside of a WHILE control structure.
3. Create a list variable named payroll to store employee names and salaries.
4. When "A" is selected the program should as for the employee name and salary.
5. When "R" is selected, the program should ask for the employee ID to be removed. If an incorrect ID is informed a warning message should be printed.

Solution

#	Algorithm 6.25
01	`payroll = []`
02	`stay = True`
03	
04	`while stay:`
05	`    print("---------------------------------")`
06	`    print("<A>dd, <R>emove, <L>ist, or <E>xit? ")`
07	`    option = input()`
08	`    print("---------------------------------")`
09	`    if option == "E":`
10	`        stay=False`
11	`    elif option == "A":`
12	`        print("Name: ")`
13	`        name = input()`
14	`        print("Salary:")`
15	`        salary = int(input())`
16	`        payroll.append( [name,salary] )`
17	`    elif option == "R":`
18	`        print("Enter employee ID #")`
19	`        i = int(input())`
20	`        if len(payroll) >= i:`
21	`            payroll.pop(i)`
22	`            print("Employee sucessuly removed")`
23	`        else:`
24	`            print("ID # not found")`
25	`    elif option == "L":`
26	`        total = 0`
27	`        for i, employee in enumerate(payroll):`
28	`            name = employee[0]`
29	`            salary = employee[1]`
30	`            print(i, name, salary)`
31	`            total += salary`
32	`        print("Total:",total)`
33	
34	`print("Program ended")`
35	
	The salary of John is 45000

1. Execute Algorithm 6.25 for testing and analysis.

.

CHAPTER 7

Wrap Up

Well, here you are! Congratulations, you did it! But, you know, it is not the end of your journey, it is the end of a cycle. You are still there, in your journey. However, better prepared than before to start new cycles and keep going.

Studying the chapters of this book, you had the opportunity to discuss the importance of computers for the personal and business base. Now you are aware that almost everything today is digitally connected because computers are becoming more powerful, smaller, and affordable each year. Also, you learned: computer as an electronic device has been used for people from different generations; computers are present everywhere and have been employed for various purposes like study, work, and entertainment, to mention a few. Consequently, more and more companies can invest in more technology. This fact explains why computers play an essential role in business today, helping organizations to be more efficient and competitive. Investing in technology, companies can do more with less.

Also, you learned how important it is to understand computers and all those stuff related to technology. Being the technology more and more present in the workplace, companies need professionals well qualified. Those professionals need more skills related to computers to manage and operate business functions efficiently throughout modern technology. That is why, if you want to succeed in a professional career today, you have to be more than just a computer user. What you have to do is fundamentally understand how to use computers as a professional tool.

Understanding the difference between hardware and software is a good beginning. You could learn: almost everything played every day for any organization will include some use of computers; a computer is a system that receives information from the input, processes that information, and returns the output as a result; a computer is a machine that converts data into information; computers are getting smaller and less expensive every day; modern technology helps the firm to be more efficient; personal computers include desktops, notebooks, and mobile devices. Now, after going through the content of this book, reading, discussing, answering the questions, and solving the proposed problems, you learned more. You got it, and you have a better comprehension of how a computer system works in an organization. Also, you probably can present reasons to explain the importance of the local network as well as the Internet.

You had a lot of practice! Moving files, sending e-mails, storing and sharing files on the cloud. These are just simple tasks executed every day for anyone working in the business area. But, you did more. You created a flyer, resume, letter, order, report, and presentations. Working on these projects, you had the opportunity to use the Microsoft Office as a business professional. Doing these activities helped you to realize: Microsoft Office 2019 is a crucial software suite to help companies make more easy task management and, as a result, get things done more efficiently; Microsoft Word is a word processing program designed to help you create professional-quality documents; Excel is a spreadsheet editor that allows you to create tables, calculate and analyze data; and PowerPoint is a widely used application for developing presentations. So, you are ready to go forward and work on projects more challenging.

Certainly, the most challenging part of this book was programming. Completing the last chapter you could learn: Python is a programming language created in the late 1980s by Guido van Rossum and can be used for the development of desktop and Web solutions; Kaggle is a free platform and an online community of data scientists and machine learning practitioners; a variable is an object or memory address capable of retaining and representing a value or expression; operators are symbols that tell the Python interpreter to do some mathematical or logical operation; a control structure (or flow of control) refers to the order in which instructions, expressions, and function calls are executed or evaluated; a function is a block of organized and reusable code used to perform a specific action, only running when it is called; a class describes the actions of its objects and what information they can store; Pandas is a library that provides structures and data analysis tools. You had to work hard on the understanding of how to create computer programs. But, doing this, you were able to experience how useful and powerful a computer can be. Using your creativity, you can solve complex problems. This kind of skill for a business professional is an asset.

1. Keep this book for future reference. You can come back to this any time to refresh your memory or to remember any forgotten concept.

References

Castells, M. 2005. *The Network Society: A Cross-Cultural Perspective*. Edward Elgar.

Esteras, S.R. 2013. *Infotech English for Computer Users*. Cambridge, UK: Cambridge University Press.

Jadhav, S.S. 2009. *Advanced Computer Architecture and Computing*. Technical Publications.

Merriam-Webster.com Dictionary. https://merriam-webster.com/ (accessed March 14, 2020).

McKinney, W., and P.D. Team. 2020. *Pandas—Powerful Python Data Analysis Toolkit*.

Ribeiro, S.S. 2019. "Issues of Strategic Digital City." *Urban Science* 3, no. 4, p. 102.

Zimmermann, K.A. 2017. "History of Computers: A Brief Timeline." *LiveScience. Purch*, https://livescience.com/20718-computer-history.html (accessed on September 7, 2017).

About the Author

Dr. Sergio S. Ribeiro is an assistant professor of business administration at Briercrest College and Seminary. He holds a PhD in Urban Management, with an emphasis on the evidence-based decision process in strategic digital city. His master's degree is in computer science with a specialization in computer vision, data mining, and artificial intelligence. Graduated in business administration and information technology, he has a postgraduate certificate in education. Also, he worked more than 20 years in the industry developing software solutions as well as acting in business process automation.

Index

www.ingramcontent.com/pod-product-compliance
Lightning Source LLC
Chambersburg PA
CBHW050501190326
41458CB00005B/1388